Principles of Human Development: An analysis of aggression in children and adolescents based on the theoretical framework of Piaget, Vygotsky, and Bandura

READS
178

1 AUTHOR:

Ethel Fay Okocha
AMERICAN INTERNATIONAL SCHOOL OF EGYPT...

Available from: Ethel FAY Okocha
Retrieved on: 02 April 2016

Principles of Human Development: An analysis of aggression in children and adolescents based on the theoretical framework of Piaget, Vygotsky, and Bandura.

Journal:	Management in Education
Manuscript ID:	MIE-10-013
Manuscript Type:	Original Manuscript
Keywords:	onset of aggression, childhood and youth aggression, Piaget, Vygotsky, and Bandura, Principles of child development, school violence

ABSTRACT
Breadth

Working within the theoretical framework of child growth and development, the work of three classical theorists will be analyzed in this breadth paper, including Jean Piaget, Albert Bandura, and Lev Vygotsky, in order to examine the development of cognition, personality, and self-efficacy and how they relate to behavior in children and adolescents. A critical analysis contrasting their views regarding the development of personality and self-efficacy will also be included.

ABSTRACT
Depth

Quality of life is directly correlated with creating a safe environment that is not characterized by fear and intimidation in neighborhoods, schools, and places of employment.

These places where people carry on their lives have become inundated by violent youth, and all stakeholders must become proactive in identifying youth who exhibit aggressive, violent behavior. The earlier that people identify the underlying causes of these aggressive behaviors and implement intervention strategies, the sooner these senseless acts of violence can be reduced. Working within the theoretical framework of child growth and development, the depth component of KAM II will examine current research studies in order to explore the onset of aggressive behavior in children to identify developmental factors that contribute to aggressive behavior and to determine if biological predictors indicate a genetic basis of aggression.

ABSTRACT
Application

School safety is a critical prerequisite to raising academic achievement. A school's climate is directly associated with levels of aggression and violence as well as high levels of academic excellence. This application project examines school climate and synthesizes best practices utilized to facilitate effective school-based violence prevention. Criteria are utilized to assess a school-based intervention plan currently utilized in ten of the most violent secondary Chicago public schools.

Main Document

Core Knowledge Area Module 2:

Principles of Human Development

Program: PhD in Education

Specialization: K-12 Educational Leadership

ABSTRACT

Breadth

Working within the theoretical framework of child growth and development, the work of three classical theorists will be analyzed in this breadth paper, including Jean Piaget, Albert Bandura, and Lev Vygotsky, in order to examine the development of cognition, personality, and self-efficacy and how they relate to behavior in children and adolescents. A critical analysis contrasting their views regarding the development of personality and self-efficacy will also be included.

ABSTRACT

Depth

Quality of life is directly correlated with creating a safe environment that is not characterized by fear and intimidation in neighborhoods, schools, and places of employment. These places where people carry on their lives have become inundated by violent youth, and all stakeholders must become proactive in identifying youth who exhibit aggressive, violent behavior. The earlier that people identify the underlying causes of these aggressive behaviors and implement intervention strategies, the sooner these senseless acts of violence can be reduced. Working within the theoretical framework of child growth and development, the depth component of KAM II will examine current research studies in order to explore the onset of aggressive behavior in children to identify developmental factors that contribute to aggressive behavior and to determine if biological predictors indicate a genetic basis of aggression.

ABSTRACT

Application

School safety is a critical prerequisite to raising academic achievement. A school's climate is directly associated with levels of aggression and violence as well as high levels of academic excellence. This application project examines school climate and synthesizes best practices utilized to facilitate effective school-based violence prevention. Criteria are utilized to assess a school-based intervention plan currently utilized in ten of the most violent secondary Chicago public schools.

TABLE OF CONTENTS

ABSTRACTS
- Breadth — i
- Depth — ii
- Application — iii

BREADTH
- Introduction — 1
- Lev Vygotsky — 3
- Jean Piaget — 8
- Albert Bandura — 12
- Synthesis of Cognitive Development Theories — 16
- Comparison and Contrast of Theories — 20
- Development of Adolescence Self Efficacy — 21
- Conclusion — 23

DEPTH
- Annotated Bibliography — 25
- Literature Review Essay Introduction — 55
    - Developmental Pathways of Aggression and Violence — 57
    - Onset of Aggression — 58
    - Risk Factors that Contribute to Aggression — 61
    - Biological Predictors of Aggression — 71
    - Correlates of Violent Behaviors in School Settings — 73
    - Conclusion — 75

APPLICATION
- Introduction — 77
- School Climate — 79
- Legal Issues and Students' Rights — 85
- School-Based Violence Prevention — 86
- Action Plan to Improve School Climate — 96
- Conclusion — 98

REFERENCES — 100

SBSF 8210   Theories of Human Development

Introduction

In an attempt to understand the knowledge acquisition of Homo sapiens and how this acquisition influences behavior, various theories about human development have evolved. These theories transcend the philosophical realm into the psychological realm. Initially, the philosopher Plato (427-347 B.C.) suggested two sources of knowledge—sensory and intellectual (Crombie, 1962). Aristotle (384-522 B.C.), his protégé, agreed, but Aristotle believed that intellectual data could be retrieved or abstracted from the senses (McKeon, 1941). A subsequent thinker, G.W. F. Hegel (1770-1831) proposed that all human development began in the mind. He utilized his dialectical method to explain mental growth and transformations. However, ideas and philosophical theorizing always appear to succumb to science methodology. In the early 1900s, psychologists began to conduct research studies focusing on child growth and development in order to understand knowledge acquisition. As a result, two major schools of thought emerged: behaviorism and cognitivism.

Behaviorism is a branch of psychology that focuses on activities that can be observed and measured (Watson, 1919). No concern is given to the brain or underlying thought processes that facilitate learning. John B. Watson is credited as the founder and B.F. Skinner as his most noteworthy protégé. Skinner's experiments on operant conditioning utilizing rats as test subjects and Watson's supposition that learning only occurs when there are measurable changes in performance made the behaviorist model the order of the day. Forty years later in 1950, behaviorism began to lose its momentum. Noam Chomsky, a linguist, began analyzing language acquisition in children and the mental structures involved. Chomsky believed that behaviorism could not explain the internal, rule governing process. However, cognitivism or cognitive science attempts to explain the nature of human intelligence and how it works by studying the mind (Anderson, 2000). Its underlying premise is that the learner is an active agent, storing information in the brain in an organized manner, not as a passive object as in behaviorism. Cognition proposes a theory of learning that extends beyond observations of external behavior and encompasses conceptual knowledge, short and long term memory, and addresses divergent learning styles. Chomsky and others concluded that language is a primary cognitive function because language and logic are interdependent (Bruner, 1977; Chomsky, 1959; & McNamara, 1972).

Lev Vygotsky (1896-1934), Jean Piaget (1896-1980) and Albert Bandura (1924-) are the three major theorists in cognitive psychology. These three theorists have been chosen for this KAM because their research is applicable today, because they relate behavior to the developmental processes of children. Devotion and dedication to children is a central theme that permeates the work of these theorists. They are developmental psychologists, believing that intelligence in children develops in stages. However, they differ in the manner in which they analyze how children's lower order mental processes are transformed into adult higher order mental processes. Piaget's model described children's stages of cognitive development from birth to young adult, while Vygotsky believed that development is a continuous process that begins at birth and ends at death. Vygotsky also believed that development is too complex to designate by stages of development. Bandura is a modern day cognitive psychologist whose theories synthesized the work of Vygotsky and Piaget. Bandura and Vygotsky both emphasize the importance of social learning in child growth and development. Bandura recently renamed his social learning theory as social cognitive theory due to the limitations imposed by his own title. His current research deals with motivational factors and self-regulatory mechanisms. In essence, all three men have made significant contributions to educational, developmental, and cognitive psychology.

This paper will explore child growth and development and the theories of these three classical theorists as their work relates to the development of cognition, personality, and self-efficacy in children and adolescents. The paper will conclude with a critical child development.

Lev Semenovich Vygotsky

In order to fully comprehend Vygotsky's philosophy, ideologies, and theories, one must attempt to understand the historical and social context in which these developed. Vygotsky was born in pre-revolutionary Russia on November 5, 1886 to a middle class Jewish family. In 1887, approximately a year after his birth, Vygotsky's father, an executive banker, moved his family from Orsha to Gomel. Gomel was a restricted territory for Jewish families who had been expelled from the city of Moscow and other villages (Brecher, 1995). The progroms, the Temporary Laws of May, 1882, and other anti-Jewish repressive policies of the imperialist regime of Nicholas and Alexandra forced Jewish people to relocate (Blanck, 1984). Jewish families refused to abandon their religious practices and would not assimilate into the mainstream. Due to the restrictive educational policies that were enacted, Vygotsky received his primary education at home. Vygotsky's tutor, Solomon Ashpia, taught Vygotsky lessons using a technique based on Socratic dialogues, while his mother instructed him in German and

French (Vyygodskaya, 1984). By the age of 15, Vygotsky could speak and write German, Russian, Hebrew, English, Latin, and Greek. He was called the "little professor.' By 1913 Vygotsky completed prepatory studies and applied to Moscow University. University admissions restricted Jewish students to 3% of the total population; however, he was accepted. Vygotsky's desired field of study was history, which was prohibited because it led to a teaching career, and Jewish people were not allowed to hold such positions. Therefore, Vygotsky entered medical school, where he stayed one month and switched to law school. While in attendance at Moscow University, Vygotsky also gained admission to Shaniavsky People's University. This university was created in 1906 by Alfonso Shaniavsky, when leading scholars were expelled from Moscow's Imperial University following a revolt against the czar (Blanck, 1984). While in attendance at Shaniavsky, philosophy became Vygotsky's favorite subject. He began reading great literary works by Hegel, Marx, and Engel, formulating his own philosophy of man. It was also at this university that Vygotsky heard his first psychology lectures (Kozulin, 1986). Vygotsky was awarded degrees from both universities at the age of 21. In 1917 he returned to his hometown Gomel, following an October socialist revolution in which restrictions were lifted, and Jewish people were allowed to participate in all areas of Russian life (Wertsh, 1985). Vygotsky began teaching and lecturing in Gomel and other parts of Russia. Even though he became a major figure in Gomel, economic conditions were terrible. In 1919 Vygotsky contracted tuberculosis, which would eventually lead to his demise fifteen years later.

Psychology was Vygotsky's major focus by the time he married Rosa Noevna

Smekhove in 1924 who was a caretaker for mentally and physically disabled children. Even though he had no formal training in psychology, it was during this time frame that Pedagogical Institute in Gomel. He obtained data for his first major research project. In 1925 he completed and submitted "The Psychology of Art" as his doctoral dissertation to the Moscow Institute of Psychology, even though he was hospitalized with tuberculosis which prevented him from defending it (Vygodsky, 1984). While hospitalized, he also wrote his controversial essay, "Historical Meaning of the Crisis in Psychology", which analyzed the divisive state of psychology. Vygotsky felt that there were too many divisions utilizing the label psychology that were more related to philosophy and the humanities than science.

Between 1922 and 1926, Vygotsky's writings dealt with the education of special needs children and other problems in education. In 1925 he became the first director of the Psychology Laboratory for Abnormal Childhood in Moscow, presently the Institute of Defectology of the Academy of Pedagogical Sciences (Blanck, 1984). Between 1925 until his death in 1930, Vygotsky held many influential positions and trained many psychologists and teachers. The three major areas he influenced were educational psychology, psychopathology, and studies involving special needs children. However, in his lasts years, his research focus was the development of cognitive structures and the higher order mental processes involved in decision making, memory, and language comprehension of people from other cultures. However, this research was stifled again by the politics of Stalin.

Karl Marx (1819-1893) and Friedrich Engels (1820-1895) provide the philosophical backdrop for Vygotsky's sociohistorical model of psychology. In Vygotsky's (1930) journal article, "The Socialist Alteration of Man", he extensively quoted Marx and Engels, embracing their socialist ideology that through socialism society's ills would be resolved (Van der Veer & Valsiner, 1994). Vygotsky stated, "A fundamental change of the whole system of those relationships which man is a part of, will also inevitably lead to a change in man's whole behavior" (p. 181). In the same article, Vygotsky dismissed Friedrich Nietzsche's overman (superman) theory regarding man's transformation into an independent, higher level being, free of modern society's values and religion. According to Vygotsky, Nietzsche's theory was flawed due to his point of reference. In 1930, Vygotsky responded with the following:

> This theory is erroneous, because it ignores the fact that the laws of historical evolution of man differ fundamentally from the laws of biological evolution and that the basic difference between these two processes consists of the fact that a human being evolves and develops as a historical, social being. Only a raising of all humanity to a higher level in social life, the liberation of all of humanity, can lead to the formation of a new type of man. (Moll, 2004, p. 182)

Working within this philosophical context, Vygotsky conducted experiments observing normal and special needs children, yielding data that eventually resulted in a rift between his colleagues. Vygotsky abandoned the zoological model (Kohler, 1921) of child development, formulating his own principles. Vygotsky believed that biological and cognitive development in children does not occur in isolation, but are interdependent and dominated by "cultural behavior supplied by the environment" (Van Der Veer & Valsiner, 1994, pp. 99). According to Vygotsky, during infancy biological reflexes dominate until maturation when they are replaced by social experiences. Vygotsky labeled this period the sociogenesis of psychological phenomena. He posited, "All higher mental functions originate in the social environment" (Vygotsky, 1926, 1993, p. 58). These principles form the basic theoretical framework of Vygotsky's social development theory. His theory states that cognitive development in children is determined by their social interactions with adults. Adults socialize children into their respective cultures by utilizing tools of that culture. These tools are usually verbal (speech and language) and non-verbal (gestures) that are used to function within their environment. Internalization of these tools leads to higher thinking skills. This process is termed the Zone of Proximal Development (ZPD). Vygotsky defined ZPD as: "the distance between the actual development levels as determined by independent problem solving and the level of potential development as determined through problem solving under adult guidance or in collaboration with more capable peers" (Vygotsky, 1978, p.50). The difference between the actual developmental levels is the ZPD. Vygotsky (1934) stated that there are four stages within the ZPD, characterized by the following: Stage I occurs when the child is given instructions and an adult or capable peer models the task on a higher developmental level. Open dialogue must ensue during task performance. Stage II occurs when the child engages in the task without assistance and uses self-directed speech for self-guidance. Stage III occurs when the child executes task without assistance. During this phase performance is developed. Stage IV occurs when assistance is given only when requested by the child.

In order to improve the quality of classroom instruction, emphasis has been placed on fewer teacher directed instructions in lieu of more student-teacher collaboration, cognitively guided instruction, and peer tutoring. Vygotsky's four stages of the ZPD have facilitated a profound change in educational institutions and in reciprocal teaching. The three R"s of reading, 'riting, and 'rithmetic have been replaced with the new three R's of rigor, relevancy, and relationships.

Today, Vygotsky's popularity is increasing, and his writings have been translated from Russian to various languages around the world. During the Stalinist regime, over 180 of his works were banned and did not resurface until the late 1960s (Moll, 2000). Vygotsky, who completed the majority of his research in education and had no formal training in psychology, is now ranked among the top psychologists in the world. His socio-historical psychology model has had a major impact in psychology, special education, and general education.

Jean Piaget

The name of Swiss born Jean Piaget (1896-1980) is synonymous with child psychology and cognitive development. Piaget's observational research laid a foundation that delineates stages of development in children and identifies characteristics of how information is processed at each stage. Jean Piaget's theoretical framework of child growth and development is constructivist and based on genetic epistemology. His theory takes a biological approach, focusing on the physical development of a child as well as the mental development, believing both are progressive, continuous processes that are not always aligned. Piaget (1968) stated:
Genetic epistemology attempts to explain knowledge, and in particular, scientific knowledge, on the basis of its history, its sociogenesis, and especially the psychological origins of the notions and operations upon which it is based. It takes into account

logical formalizations applied to equilibrated thought structures and in certain cases to transformations from one level to another in the development of thought (p. 64). Piaget believed that "cognitive processes reflect autoregulatory mechanisms that are evident at the organic level" (Piaget, 1974, p.8). Genes, heredity, and environment interact during development, and a process of equilibration facilitates this interaction. Piaget contended that "the mind facilitates survival by maintaining a physiological and psychological mediated dynamic equilibrium with its environment" (Piaget, 1968, p. 103). It is the process that describes cognition and cognitive development. Equilibration occurs in three phases: assimilation, accommodation, and adaptation. According to Piaget (1968), "Assimilation is the process of absorbing and organizing experiences around the activities that produce them" (p.12). Initially, assimilation is characterized by an infant's physical response to external stimuli by smiling, making various vocalizations, and tracking sounds and people with eye-head movements and other non-verbal cues. During the developmental cycle, non-verbal responses lead to verbal responses. Assimilation is continuous throughout a person's lifetime and is constantly modified by accommodation. Accommodation occurs when assimilated experiences are integrated into a child's repertoire. Piaget (1977) described this process as follows: "Many situations or objects resist the activity patterns the child tries on them, and in so doing impose some changes on these patterns themselves. Still others yield new results which go to enrich the range or scope of the patterns" (p.9). Adaptation is the great equalizer of assimilation and accommodation. It is the final process that controls or modifies behaviors based on information that has been processed. These three steps of equilibration form the basic concept of Piaget's epistemology.

Piaget's theory of cognitive development suggests that infants enter the world with no pre-existing cognitive competences. They must pass through four stages of development acquiring various skill sets. Piaget's four stages are the *Sensorimotor Period, Preoperational Stage, Concrete Operations*, and *Formal Operations.* These stages are age specific and identifiable utilizing various tasks.

The *Sensorimotor Period* encompasses birth to two years of age when an infant interacts with the environment via their five senses. Tactile, auditory, and visual stimulation are crucial to development. Infants visually track people and objects with their eyes, exhibit auditory stimulation by localizing the direction of sounds and are soothed by gentle touching. This stage is characterized by specific developmental milestones such as crawling, sitting up with/without assistance, and basic vocalizations like crying and sucking noises that progress to monosyllabic utterances or the beginning of speech. The specific task Piaget associated with this time frame is *Object Permanence*. Piaget concluded from his experiments that an infant will visually attend and reach for an object until a cloth is placed over it. When the object is covered and no longer in visual range, the infant appears to loose the hidden object.

The *Preoperational Stage* extends from 2 to 7 years of age and exhibits how children progress in their understanding of space, time, quantity, movement, and speed. Representational skills along with language skills are developing. Egocentric speech develops during this stage. The specific task for this stage is *conservation.* The child is presented with two rows of objects lined up that contain the same quantity (i.e. crayons or pieces of candy). One row is compressed, so that it appears shorter and the second row is spaced, so that it appears longer. The child is asked to identify the row that has more objects. A child under six years of age will say the longer row automatically by relying on visual cues. A more mature, cognitively developed child will count the objects in each row before providing an answer. Piaget also utilized liquids to display conservation by pouring the same amount of liquid into two beakers. One beaker is tall and slim, and the other beaker is short and wide. When the child is asked to identify the beaker with more liquid, the younger child will not hesitate to identify the tallest beaker. The more mature, cognitively developed child will verbalize doubts regarding the taller beaker and choose the short, wide one instead.

Thought processes are more organized from age 7 to 12 years of age and language skills have advanced and are used to communicate with other people during the *Concrete Operational Stage.* The child is interacting within a larger, more complex environment. Piaget asserted that, at the completion of this stage, a child has attained "a system of class concepts and relations; arithmetic operations (addition, multiplication, etc., and their inverses); geometric operations (sections, displacements, etc.); temporal operations (seriation of events, i.e., the successive ordering of events and the nesting of intervals between them); mechanical operations; physical operations, etc." (p. 48). During this stage, the specific tasks are those introduced in the other stages. The child should be able to pass all related tasks.

Piaget's ultimate stage of development, *Formal Operations* from ages 12 to adulthood is the completion of all prior stages resulting in a culmination of a new structure of thought called formal thought. This transformation allows adolescents to partake in logical, abstract thinking. The adolescent is capable of reasoning, hypothesizing, and drawing conclusions. Piaget (1968) stated that some adolescents will never attain this level. Only during this final stage of cognitive development does a child reach equilibrium. It marks the completion of all operational and logical structures.

Analogous to Piaget's stages of development is language acquisition that Piaget believed is basic to cognitive development because it facilitates thought and logic. Piaget (1968) stated that this language acquisition has three consequences that are essential to mental development: (1) the possibility of verbal exchange with other persons, which heralds the onset of socialization of action; (2) the internalization of words, i.e., the appearance of thought itself, supported by internal language and a system of signs; and (3) the internalization of action as such which from now on, rather than being purely perceptual and motor as it has been, can represent itself intuitively by means of pictures and mental experiments (p.17). Thus, Piaget's research into the developmental processes of children and how they process information has laid a foundation for child psychologists and educators to follow for years to come. Piaget revolutionized child psychology with his theory of cognitive development.

Albert Bandura

Bandura began teaching and conducting psychological research at Stanford University in 1953. Initially, his research focus was on aggressive behaviors and social learning. As a result of his research studies involving aggressive, hostile, adolescents, Bandura published his first book in 1959 titled *Adolescent Aggression*. During this time frame, Bandura developed his theory of reciprocal determinism, which was later named triadic reciprocality. This theory states that human influence interacting with the environment is not a unilateral process. A person's behavior may be the result of interactions within his or her environment, but the person's response may facilitate a change in the environment (Bandura, 1959). In 1960, Bandura's work with children led to the development of his social learning theory. Bandura's (1977) theoretical framework is based on the following three ideas: (a) the possibility of verbal exchange with other persons, which heralds the onset of socialization of action, (b) the internalization of words, i.e., the appearance of thought itself, supported by internal language and a system of signs, and (c) the internalization of action as such which from now on, rather than being purely perceptual and motor as it has been, can represent itself intuitively by means of pictures and mental experiments. Bandura (1977) also believed that through the social learning theory "human nature is characterized as a vast potentiality that can be fashioned by direct and vicarious experience into a variety of forms within biological limits" (p. 13). The social learning theory explains human behavior as "a continuous reciprocal interaction between cognitive, behavioral, and environmental influences" (Bandura, 1977, p. 17). This is a revised definition of Bandura's social learning theory, because prior to 1977, the word "cognitive" was not included. Bandura outlined three basic processes inherent in his social learning theory: observation, identification, and imitation. Bandura (1977) stated that observational learning encompasses the following: (a) attention which includes modeled events and observer characteristics, (b) retention which includes symbolic coding, cognitive organization, and motor rehearsal, (c) motor reproduction which includes physical capabilities, self-observation of reproduction, and accuracy of feedback, and (d) motivation including external, vicarious, and self-reinforcement.

    Bandura explained that when a child learns a new behavior, first he/she attends to the person exhibiting the desired behavior. During this time, the child will ignore any distracting environmental stimuli, only focusing on the model. Next, the child must be able to differentiate aspects of his/her behavior with that of the model. Positive motivation must be present at this step, because the behavior attempting to be duplicated must appear relevant to the child. Bandura explained that when a child is learning a new behavior, first he/she attends to the person exhibiting the desired behavior. During this time, the child will ignore any distracting environmental stimuli, only focusing on the model. Next, the child must be able to differentiate aspects of his/her behavior with that of the model. Positive motivation must be present at this step, because the behavior attempting to be duplicated must appear relevant to the child. Bandura (1977) argued, "The functional value of the behaviors displayed by different models is therefore highly influential in determining which models people will observe and which they will disregard, because the child must be able to interpret the model's behavior in some symbolic way" (p. 24). Bandura (1977) also asserted that the child must have acquired some level of linguistic sophistication in order to comprehend explanations because "observers' capacities to process information govern how much they will benefit from observed experiences. Children retain new behaviors by mentally and physically rehearsing them. Images that have been stored may be ascertained through image recall and rehearsed mentally or physically, imitating the actual behavior. Even though all three processes are important, Bandura asserted that, during child growth and development, the strongest of these processes is imitation. Imitation facilitates the acquisition of "an array of responses that are new and unfamiliar to the child" (Bandura, 1977, p.42). According to social learning theory, these responses are reinforced differently at various stages of the child's development. When children are younger,

Bandura believed that control is physical and external. Bandura (1977) stated, "In attempting to discourage hazardous conduct in children who have not yet learned to talk, parents must resort to physical intervention. As children mature, social sanctions increasingly replace physical ones" (p.43). Bandura also believed that there is a moral component inherits in social sanctions that children master as they develop. Bandura (1977) stated:

> During the course of development, children also learn how to get around moral consequences. They discover they can avoid, or reduce reprimands by invoking extenuating circumstances for their conduct. As a result, different types of vindications become salient cues for moral judgments. ...A theory of moral reasoning must therefore be equally concerned with the cognitive processes by which the immoral can be made moral. (p.44)

Bandura also acknowledged that models, whether they are in the child's immediate environment or on television, play an important role in this moral component. Bandura (1977) stated, "To the developing child, televised modeling, which dramatizes a vast range of moral conflicts, constitutes another integral part of social learning" (p.44). According to Bandura, models in children's environment influence their thoughts and behavior patterns. Thus, Bandura's social learning theory encompasses cognitive determinants, which led him to revise his theory. Bandura's social-cognitive theory is more accurate.

    Bandura's social-cognitive theory is relevant today because it addresses moral development in children with cognitive development in children. Bandura provided explanations to questions regarding aggressive behaviors in children and offered suggestions that facilitate implementation of individual and social safeguards necessary for survival. Bandura, Piaget, and Vygotsky provide a wealth of knowledge regarding how children grow and develop cognitive abilities; however, Bandura took the collective research to another level, at another angle. Bandura (1977) argued, "As a science concerned with the social consequences of its applications, psychology must promote public understanding of psychological issues that bear on social policies to ensure that its findings are used in the service of human betterment" (p. 213).

Synthesis of the Cognitive Development Theories

The developmental process of children does not occur in a vacuum. Children develop physically and mentally within a cultural context characterized by social mores, economic status, and language. These factors comprise the child's environment and facilitate cognitive growth and development. Culture is that learned part of the environment that is transmitted by others within the group, and its biological basis is the same for all children in society. It is the result of the child interacting with biological and environmental stimuli. Piaget (1967) argued, "At birth mental life is limited to the exercise of reflex apparatus… and motor coordination that corresponds to instinctual needs such as nutrition" (p.9). In *Tool and Symbol in Child Development*, Vygotsky (1934) suggested that "in the essence of those forms of infant behavior, characteristic of the earliest stage of development, it must be noted that the child enters into relations with the situation not directly, but through the medium of another person" (p. 115). Bandura (1977) also stated, "Biological factors, of course play a role in the acquisition process" (p.16). Vygotsky, Piaget, and Bandura agreed that environment is crucial at each stage of a child's development. However, Vygotsky (1935) also stipulated that environment, " should not be regarded as a condition of development which purely objectively determines the development of a child by virtue of the fact that it contains certain qualities or features, but one should always approach environment from the point of view of the relationship which exists between the child and its environment at a given stage of his development" (p. 338).

Vygotsky (1978) also outlined four developmental stages that characterize a child's mastery over his or her environment that result in self-regulation. In reference to an essay written by Vygotsky titled *The Genesis of Higher Mental Functions* (1960/1981), Diazn, Neal and Williams (2005) outlined these stages: (a) *Stage I or A Stage of Natural and Primitive Responses*. This stage is characterized by children who master and eventually become independent of their stimulus field, (b) *Stage II or Child is Capable of Mediation Using External Sig* and its environment at a given stage of his development. This stage occurs when the child begins to mediate the environment by utilizing signs as an aid as to his or her responses and, and (c) *Stage III or Children Begin to Manipulate Signs*. In order to achieve a given desired response, the child will regulate his or her own behavior, and (d) *Stage IV or Developmental Progression toward Self-Regulation*. This stage is characterized by the internalization of the external relations among stimuli, signs, and behavior. These stages indicate the use of tools by children to manipulate their environment, in order that they can gain freedom from the stimulus field. Tools such as words facilitate cognition. Vygotsky, Piaget, and Bandura agreed that speech is a tool and like the environment, a correlative of cognitive development.

Thus, Piaget, Bandura, and Vygotsky agreed that language acquisition facilitates cognitive development, and it is the primary indicator of a child's level of cognitive development (Piaget, 1964; Bandura, 1992; Vygotsky, 1990). All three men believed that language development is directly correlated with thought and that one precedes the other. Piaget (1968) asserted that "through the influence of language and socialization, intelligence is transformed during early childhood from simple sensorimotor or practical intelligence to thought itself" (p.22). However, Bandura and Vygotsky strongly disagreed with Piaget's description of the purpose of children's egocentric speech and the time frame in which it occurs during language development. When Piaget conducted studies to support his view of egocentrism during the preoperational stage of cognitive development in children, he stated that, during this stage, children focus on themselves and are incapable of doing otherwise. This stage is characterized by egocentric speech that disappears as the child grows older and does not provide communication (Piaget, 1926). Vygotsky (1934) duplicated Piaget's experiment to obtain a better understanding of egocentric speech. Vygotsky (1934) concluded that "the data obtained led us to a new comprehension of this phenomenon that differs greatly from that of Piaget. Our investigation suggests that egocentric speech does play a specific role in the child's activity" (p. 29). Vygotsky (1929) also concluded, "The most important stage in the development of reasoning and speech is the transition from external to internal speech" (p. 68). Regarding Bandura and language development, Bandura (1977) could not utilize imitation to explain transformational grammar, but he weakly postulated, "Whatever the innate potentiality may be, few would question that social learning experiences influence the rate of language development. Rules about grammatical relations between words cannot be developed unless they are exemplified by the utterances of models" (p. 176).

Even though all three psychologists differed in their definition of cognition and at what level it takes place, they agreed that speech and language development are important components of cognitive development. Piaget, Vygotsky, and Bandura also differed in the manner that they perceived the process of cognitive development. Vygotsky believed that children construct their own cognitive reality by building on prior knowledge as they interact with their environment. Vygotsky also believed social interactions with people in their immediate environment assists in cognitive development, while Bandura believed that social learning in the environment facilitates cognitive development. Vygotsky and Bandura were critical of Piaget's theory of cognitive development. As Vygotsky (1986) stated:

> For all its greatness, Piaget's work bears the stigmata of crisis characteristic of all modern psychology. In this respect, Piaget's theory shares the fate of such theories as those of Sigmund Freud, Charles Blondel, and Lucien Levy-Bruhl. All of them are the offspring's of the crisis in psychology. This crisis stems from the sharp contradiction between the factual material of science and its methodological and theoretical premises-a contradiction deeply rooted in history of knowledge, revealing a dispute between the materialistic and idealistic world concepts. (p.13)

Clearly, Vygotsky's philosophy was the basis of this comment and should not be taken out of its historical context. During the 1930s, social transformations were taking place in the Soviet Union, and Vygotsky became dissatisfied with psychologists in general. Bandura (1977) compared his social-cognitive theory to Piaget's theory:

Both recognize the importance of sensori motor and ideomotor learning; that is young children must develop ability to translate what they perceive to corresponding actions, and to convert thought into organized sequences of actions. They differ, in however, in how representations are abstracted from exemplars and in the limiting conditions of modeling. In the social learning view, observational learning is not confined to the moderately unfamiliar. (p. 32)

Bandura (1977) also argued that Piagetian theory is limited because it relies on "self discovery through behavioral manipulation as the only source of information" (p.32). Bandura and Vygotsky's theories claimed to differ greatly from Piaget's theory, but they are similar. Their emphasis on structures, whether they are internal or external or pseudo concepts that are inductive or deductive, or involve symbolism, does not negate the underlying principle that concepts and theories evolve via the observation of children. The physical, cognitive, social, and emotional development of children is the major concern.

Comparison and Contrast of Theories

According to Piaget (1968), "personality formation begins at in middle to late childhood (eight to twelve years) with the autonomous organization of rules and values, and the affirmation of will with respect to the regulation and hierarchical organization of moral tendencies" (p. 65). Piaget (1968) also explained that "personality exists as soon as a life plan has been formed" (p.65). Piaget (1968) also clarified the time frame of personality development by stating that "now this personal system cannot be constructed prior to adolescence, because it presupposes formal thought and reflexive constructions" (p. 65). According to his theory of disequilibrium, it is precisely at this stage that disequilibrium will become flexible at every level. Bandura's personality theory is based on his principle of reciprocal determinism that stems from his social-cognitive learning theory. Thus, personality development must be a function of the individual "continuously interacting with his environment" (Bandura, 1977, p. 208). Vygotsky (1931) argued that personality development in adolescence "undergoes a real revolution" (p. 190). He believed that only in adolescence (around the age of 14 or older) does the ability to draw conclusions exist. Vygotsky (1931) stated that "thinking becomes less constrained and less concrete than the sensory source on which it is based" (p. 187). In essence, Vygotsky's (1931) personality theory argued that "the vital momentous transformations which occur in literally all parts of the adolescent's organism and personality during this crucial period, the uncovering of new deep layers of his personality...does not affect adolescent thinking. All these changes occur in other areas and spheres of the personality (p. 186).

Development of Adolescence Self-Efficacy

According to Bandura (2002), "Perceived self-efficacy is the belief in one's capabilities to organize and execute the courses of action required to manage prospective situations" (p.2). Bandura (2002) also stated that self-efficacy "involves acquiring the cognitive behavioral and self-regulating tools for creating and executing appropriate courses of action to manage ever-changing life circumstances" (p.3). Piaget (1968) described the development of adolescence self-efficacy as the "submission of self to some kind of discipline" (p. 64).

The adolescent characterizes self-efficacy as "injecting himself into adult society by projects, life plans, theoretical systems and ideas" (Piaget, 1968, p. 64).

Piaget (1968) stated that, during this period, the adolescent attains equilibrium. He also argued that "reason which expresses the highest forms of equilibrium, reunites intelligence and activity" (p.70). Vygotsky's (1931) contribution, found in his essay, *Thinking and Concept Formation in Adolescence*, stated that the adolescent "passes from thinking in complexes to thinking in concepts. This transition… signifies a real revolution in the thinking process" (as cited in Van Der Veer & Valssirer, 2000, p. 262). Bandura's (2000) writings provided procedures to strengthen adolescence self-efficacy characterized through mastery experiences or small successes, through vicarious experiences provided by role models, through social persuasion, and through structuring situations that bring success (pp.3-5).

Self-regulation and motivation are key factors of self-efficacy. When adolescents Believe they can succeed; they set high goals and then commit themselves to accomplishing them. Bandura (2003) argued that:

> Most human motivation is cognitively generated. People motivate themselves and guide their actions anticipatorily by the exercise of forethought. They form beliefs about what they can do. They anticipate likely outcomes of prospective actions. They set goals for themselves and plan courses of action designed to realize valued futures. They mobilize the resources at their command and the level of effort needed to succeed. (p.6)

Parents also are a major influence in the development of self-efficacy in their children. Those parents who maintain efficacy exhibit low stress reactions and "reduced negative emotional proclivities" (Bandura, 2000, p. 13). Since the family structure of most

American homes has changed and many children are now being raised by working mothers, the task of developing self-efficacy falls upon the schools. Most schools have positive mentor programs for students to meet and greet successful role models from their neighborhoods with whom they can identify. Depending on the level of teacher efficacy, attempts to structure successful experiences for students, along with daily, positive verbal reinforcement should be made a priority. Bandura (1977) argued that adolescents must understand that "perceived self-efficacy not only reduces anticipatory fears and inhibitions, but through expectations of eventual success, it believes they can succeed and that educators must build on their strengths, encouraging their aspirations" (p. 80).

Conclusion

Many children are growing up in environments constructed by adults who have tunnel vision. From birth to the onset of adolescence, these adult caregivers control the child's immediate environment that affects the quality of his or her life. Currently in society, a weakened family structure caused by divorce, single and uneducated mothers, not to mention the use of drugs, has separated mothers and fathers from their children, leaving them in poverty, abused, suicidal, angry, and above all hurt. These same children bring their frustrations to school, walking around full of hopelessness and rage, addressing faculty and other students with the same disrespect, callousness, and frustration they feel inside. Parents blame violence in the media and easy access to guns for the increase in violence among youth. Psychologists claim that these students are unable to control themselves, because the pre-frontal cortex of the brain that is responsible for controlling violent impulses is not fully developed until around twenty-one years of age.

Understanding human behavior is a complex task, and in an effort to make sense out of nonsense, educators and parents rely on the expertise of psychologists to define developmental parameters and provide answers to questions that facilitate a deeper understanding of these children's behavior. Utilizing their psychological theories to explain the behavior of children and adolescents, Vygotsky, Piaget, and Bandura are three theorists who have given educators and parents a point of reference to identify crucial stages of social and cognitive development in children. Their cognitive development theories have contributed substantially to the knowledge base about human development and provided insights into child development. These theorists have proven that there is a direct correlation between good quality research methodology and design. Their theories are based on continuous studies about children's learning that may assist educators and parents in their interactions with them and facilitate the educational process by providing information into how their brains process information. These theories are based on accepted principles that have been tested with children year after year. Thus, Bandura, Piaget, and Vygotsky have strengthened the intellectual capacities of children by sharing their wealth of knowledge with teachers and parents.

DEPTH

SBSF 8220 Current Research in Human Development

Annotated Bibliography

Alink, L.., Mesman, J., Zeijl, J., Stolk, M., Juffer, F., & Koot, H., et al. (2006). The early childhood aggression curve: Development of physical aggression in 10-to-50-month old children. *Child Development, 77(4)*, 954-966.

Summary

This study was based on a longitudinal research project entitled, Screening and Intervention of Problem Behavior in Toddlerhood (SCRIPT) conducted by the Centre for Child and Family Studies at Leiden University in the Netherlands. Alink et al. duplicated Tremblay's 2004 study by continuing to examine the onset of aggressive physical behavior in 10 to 50 month-old children utilizing a developmental trajectory of 12, 24, and 36 months. They modified Tremblay's 2004 experimental design, utilizing more testing instruments with additional items, interviewing both parents instead of the mother to obtain data. Infants 24 to 36 months exhibited various forms of aggressive behavior and, consistent with Treblay's findings, a rise in aggression at age 2, declining at age 4 was noted, substantiating the early development of aggression in children.

Analysis

Alink et al. duplicated Tremblay's (2004) research study identifying trajectories of physical aggression in infants within 17 to 42 months by modifying variables of the original study. Alink et al. examined the onset of physical aggression in infants at 12, 24, and 36 months and obtained reports from both parents at each stage instead of interviewing the father at the final stage. The researchers selected only Caucasian infants (n=2,253) with Dutch surnames because "sample homogeneity regarding cultural background was important" (p.

957). Demographic variables were non-existent between the infants and the educational levels of parents were no t given, but were "defined by the level of the parent with the highest education on a scale ranging from 1 to 5" (p. 958). The mean average for mothers was calculated at 3.93 and at 3.98 for fathers with a standard deviation of 1.04 for both.

The Physical Aggression Scale for Early Childhood (PASEC), was the assessment tool utilized, consisting of 11 items (8 originally from Tremblay's scale) with two additional items from the Child Behavior Checklist. These items were specifically added to explore the infants' aggressiveness towards objects and animals. Study results indicated that at 24 and 36 months, mothers and fathers reported their infants' aggressive behaviors escalated, exhibiting some form of aggressive behavior. These research findings were consistent with Tremblay's documentation of the onset of aggressive behaviors in children at approximately 7 to 12 months. Obtaining information from both parents added credibility to the data, even though the overall results substantiate Tremblay's research that aggression is evidenced in infants as early as 12 months, escalates around 24 months, and begins to decline at 36 months. The study further validates the need for early intervention programs to minimize the development of aggressive behaviors in children.

Anhalt, K., Telzrow, C., & Brown, C. (2007). Maternal stress and emotional status during the perinatal period and childhood adjustment. *School Psychology Quarterly, 22*(1), 74-90.

Summary

In this article, 948 mother-child dyads participated in this longitudinal study focusing on the effects of maternal stress during the perinatal and postnatal period on the developing child. Mothers were interviewed over a one-month following birth utilizing five indices assessing maternal separation anxiety (MSAS), parental stress (PSI), perceived social support, parental control (PLCS), and the child behavior checklist (CBCL). Subsequent data was obtained from mothers when children entered the first grade to determine the children's emotional and behavior levels. Results indicated a significant correlation between perinatal/ post-natal depression in mothers and later onset of developmental behavioral problems in their offspring. Other associated factors such as low levels of maternal education, income, and social support combined with maternal stress contributed to the behavior problems exhibited by the children. The authors also submitted an extensive literature review substantiating their hypothesis with studies that suggest maternal stress during pregnancy results in a multitude of complications for the infant including premature births, low birth weights, low apgar scores, and conduct problems that appear later in the child's development.

Analysis

This study resulted in significant support for the correlation of maternal stress during the perinatal period with potential developmental problems in children in the first grade, especially when other socioeconomic factors are considered. According to Anhalt, et al. (2007), maternal stress is associated with depressive disorders and aggression in children. The authors indicate that, "20% of randomly screened pregnant women met clinical criteria for depression" (Anhalt et al., 2007, p.85), suggesting that the numbers are probably twice as high in women from impoverished environments. Anhalt et al. postulated that during the prenatal and perinatal stages of development, depressed mothers produce "hormonal and neurochemical responses to stress, adversely and permanently altering fetal central nervous system development contributing to later psychological and behavioral outcomes" (p.76). These authors predicted that these psychological and behavioral outcomes would be evidenced in children as early as pre-school, initiating a longitudinal study focusing on 946 mother child dyads. Mothers were interviewed one month following birth, and subsequent data was obtained when the children entered the first grade. Demographics were characterized by the mothers' ethnicity, educational-level, and income-to-needs ratio. According to the authors, "all independent and dependent variables were non-categorical) except for child gender, site of data collection, and mothers' ethnicity" (p. 86). All of the assessment tools utilized indicated high internal consistency as measured by Cronbach's area of critical region. Six years later, scores were correlated from the Child Behavior Checklist (Achenbach, 1991) consisting of eight subscales measuring areas of delinquent behavior, attention problems, aggressive behavior, social problems, somatic complaints, and other areas resulted in findings that were consistent with previous studies indicating a strong link between maternal stress during the prenatal and perinatal periods and offspring that exhibit aggression and other conduct disorders.

Bonari, L., Pinto, N., Ahn, E., Einarson, A., ASteiner, M., Koren, G. (2004). Perinatal risks of untreated depression during pregnancy. *Canadian Journal of Psychiatry,* 9(11), 726-734.

Summary

The authors researched current literature from Medline and other medical sources to explore perinatal risks of untreated depression during pregnancy. Data revealed that maternal depression during this developmental period of the fetus leads to restricted fetal growth resulting in neurological damage, low birth rate, hyperactivity, attention-deficit hyperactivity disorders, and a myriad of other emotional and behavior problems. Maternal depression during the perinatal time frame may have such an adverse effect on the mother that she withdraws socially and is unable to participate in pre-natal check-ups or other available supportive services like counseling and psychotherapy. Statistical data indicated that pre-natal and post-partum maternal depression affects a large number of women who never seek help because pregnancy is supposed to be a happy time in their lives, and they feel guilty about the depression. The etiology of depression has been attributed biologically to "a hormonal problem consisting of an over activity of peptides in the hypothalamus pituitary adrenal" (p. 727) which is believed to have an effect on fetal growth. Other risks pertaining to maternal depression are noted in the research.

Analysis

Bonari et al. (2004) conducted an extensive review of the literature regarding the affects of untreated maternal depression during pregnancy, specifically during the perinatal period, revealing that depression facilitates psychopathology in their offspring along with concomitant physical problems. According to Bonari et al. (2004), data reveals that "1 in 5 pregnant women experience depression but few seek treatment" (p. 727) and "50% to 60% continue to suffer from depression in the postpartum period" (p. 731). This is serious because according to the authors' statistics, postpartum depression may account for "30,000 to 35,000 suicides yearly in North America" (Bonari et al., 2004, p. 727). Maternal depression is also correlated with developmental delays in their infants, especially when mothers exhibit postpartum depression. According to Bonari et al. (2004), "studies have found that these children are 6 times more likely to develop depression than are children of mothers without depression, suggesting that genetic susceptibility has a role, in addition to environment" (p.733). The research addresses the impact of maternal stress on the unborn fetus caused by the hypothalmo-pituitary-adrenal axis (HPA). Hyperactivity of the hypothalmo-pituitary-adrenal (HPA) axis, stimulated by stress, is characterized by preterm deliveries, low birth weight, spontaneous abortion, and other poor fetal outcomes due to hormones that cross the placenta stimulating neurotoxins during critical periods of fetal programming. In essence, the authors believe that "the biological dysregulation that occurs in depression may not be ideal for pregnancy" (Bonari et al., 2004, p. 733) and that the emotional status of pregnant women needs to be monitored as closely as their physical status within obstetrics during this critical time period.

Brennan, P., Hall, J. Bor, W., Najman, J., & Williams, G. (2003). Integrating biological and social processes in relation to early-onset persistent aggression in boys and girls. *Developmental Psychology, 39(2),* 309-323.

Summary

This article identified two developmental pathways "early-onset and late–onset" aggression, examining the biological and sociological theories of Moffitt and Patterson regarding the development of aggression. The goal of this study was to assess the associated cumulative risk factors specified by each theorist to predict which factors were most important in the identification of aggression in children and adolescents. The article also examined Aguilar's (2000) research. Participants were from a high risk sub-sample birth cohort in Australia (N = 7,775) in which the mothers reported suffering from depression during and after the birth of their children.

Analysis

The article was excellent because it outlined the two developmental pathways of childhood aggression with a brief historical analysis of the presenting theorists. One developmental pathway of early onset aggression s fetal brain damage resulting from obstetrical complications coupled with an adverse familial environment (usually poverty, low educational levels, etc.). The second developmental pathway involves late-onset aggression when adolescent youth are involved with undesirable peer groups who participate in aggressive and violent acts. This study was designed to test which pathway could accurately predict the continuity of aggression and violence from birth to adolescence. The authors cited obstetrical data for 849 boys that was taken from an ongoing longitudinal study in low-socioeconomic areas of Montreal, Canada and a SPSS statistical technique was utilized to create four obstetrical complication scales. When scores were dichotomized, preclampsia was highly correlated with later aggression and violence in children who were raised in an adverse familial environment. Teacher interviews of the boys at age six were correlated with evaluations at age 17 in which the same boys rated themselves regarding their behavior at home and school. Results indicated a direct correlation between obstetrical complications and aggression. Anyone raised in an adverse family environment will probably encounter developmental problems. However, the two developmental pathways indicated that children with obstetrical complications who are raised in adverse familial environments are more prone to aggression, leading to conduct disorders and violence in adolescence.

Brook, D., Zhang, C., Rosenberg, G., & Brook, J. (2006). Maternal cigarette smoking during pregnancy and child aggressive behavior. *The American Journal on Addiction/American Academy of Psychiatrists in Alcoholism and Addictions, 15(6), 450-456.*

Summary

This subset of participants from a longitudinal New York City study of 203 African-American and Puerto Rican eight-year-old children was utilized to examine the correlation between maternal smoking during pregnancy and aggressive behavior utilizing the OLS

(Ordinary Least Square regression analysis. Brook, Zhang, Rosenberg, and J. Brook (2006) postulated that perinatal exposure of nicotine to a developing fetus has an adverse effect and leads to aggression in childhood. Other high risk factors associated with childhood aggression were lack of maternal warmth, anti-social behavior exhibited by parents, and mothers' levels of education. Irrespective of these concomitant factors, results indicated maternal smoking during pregnancy is associated with the development of aggression in children.

Analysis

Brooks, et al. (2006) established a correlation between maternal cigarette smoking during pregnancy and the development of childhood aggression utilizing a six item rating scale. Cohen and Velez devised a scale (unpublished, 2005) with a "predictive validity" (p.452) and an internal consistency reliability of 0.78, established by using Cronbach's alpha scale. The eight-year-old participants and their mothers (mean age 29) resided in the same geographical location and attended the same school. The SAS Mixed Procedure was utilized to construct a "random linear regression model to account for the variation between families" (p. 452). Nicotine is a drug, so there has to be adverse affects associated with smoking during pregnancy. This is one of many high risk factors associated with aggression in childhood that I needed to explore.

Feder, J., Levant, R., & Dean, J. (2007). Boys and violence: A gender-informed analysis. *Professional Psychology: Research & Practice, 38*(4), 385-391.

Summary

The authors reviewed current literature on gender-based aggression, resulting in evidence substantiating the hypothesis that males more than females are socialized into aggressive behavior and violence, resulting in a high numbers of suicides. Contributing factors identified in the article were media, family involvement (directly or indirectly), peer pressure, and societal norms in general. Levant's "normative male alexithymia" was highlighted in the article, concluding with strategies to facilitate changes in our approach in developing programs with strong male mentors.

Analysis

The theoretical framework of this article is based on the premise that boys are socialized into aggression and violence, facilitated by the media, parents, peer groups, and easy access to firearms. According to Feder, Levant, and Dean (2007), "clinical and empirical research conducted over the past 2 decades has suggested that the socialization of boys to conform to traditional notions of masculinity such as toughness, aggression, dominance, and the restriction of emotional suppression may heighten the potential for boys to engage in violence" (p. 387). The authors suggested that parental influence is the major determinant of whether children develop aggressive and violent behaviors because they influence every aspect of a child's immediate environment. Parents who have a history of conduct disorders are at higher risks for modeling adverse behavior, resulting in boys who may exhibit various levels of aggression and violence. The social constructionist ideology also forms the premise of Levant's theory of normative male alexithymia, which he described as "the inability to put emotions into words" (Feder, Levant, Dean, 2007, p.390). Levant's research revealed that during the initial stages of child development, boys equal or surpass girls in emotional and physical expression of their emotions. However, by age six the language acquisition skills of boys are altered (i.e. via shaping) by parents and peers "leading boys to suppress, channel, and tune out their vulnerable emotions" (Feder,

Levant, & Dean, 2007, p. 391). Levant's researches also examined how boys are taught not to display tears or fears, but are encouraged to exhibit aggression, suggesting this is another prelude to male violence. The authors further asserted that "these results of gender role socialization predisposes boys to engage in violence" ((Feder, Levant, & Dean, 2007, p.391) which provides justification for a higher incidence of violence associated with male aggression. The authors also examined the effectiveness of male mentor programs as deterrents of aggression and violence in young males. Research results indicated that when young males bond with positive male role models, the relationships facilitate "increased self-esteem and reduced aggression" (Feder, Levant, & Dean, 2007, p.389). In essence, this article stresses the necessity of identifying potentially high-risk behaviors that contribute to aggression and violence in males and reviews the importance of implementing early intervention strategies to minimize these behaviors.

    Flanagan, K., Bierman, K., & Kam, C. (2003). Identifying at-risk children at school entry:
        The usefulness of multibehavioral problem profiles. *Journal of Clinical Child*
        and Adolescent Psychology, 32(3), 396- 407.

Summary

According to Flanagan, Bierman, and Chi-Ming Kam (2003), youth aggression is usually associated with concomitant behaviors characterized by delays in cognitive development, anti-social behavior, and hyperactivity, suggesting that screening instruments for aggression should encompass all three behaviors because they tend to overlap. The focus of this study was to predict the reliability and validity of utilizing several screening instruments as opposed to one, when assessing high-risk aggressive children. Participants were randomly selected from a pre-existing longitudinal study on the development and prevention of conduct disorders in which 755 middle-income children from North

Carolina, Tennessee, Washington, and Pennsylvania had been identified as high risk. Children from various ethnic backgrounds were selected from each state and evaluated with three different assessments. Scores were dichotomized, those above the cutoff score were deemed problematic, and behavior indicators were utilized to construct predictive behavior profiles. Results utilizing the three assessments that focused on student profiles indicated that high aggression in first graders was highly predictive of aggression in those same students in third grade, substantiating the researchers' theory that "the efficacy of early screening strategies might be increased by considering multi-problem profiles exhibited by young children" (p. 397).

Analysis

This study proved that utilizing multiple screening instruments increases the reliability and validity of data collected in the early identification of aggression in children. Initially, teachers rated their first grade children, and two years later, they rated the same children in third grade, utilizing a battery of assessment tools: the *Teacher Checklist* (Dodge & COIE, 1987), the *Social Health Profile* (CPPRG, 1997), the *Attention Deficit Hyperactivity Disorder Checklist* (DuPaul, 1990), and cumulative grades assessing levels of hyperactivity, prosocial deficits, and aggression. Sociometric interviews were conducted with children individually with a person-oriented approach because the researchers believed that this approach "examines the influence of behavior problems in their intrapersonal context, in contrast to variable-oriented approaches that explore the general predictability of behavioral dimensions in a sample (Flanagan et al., 2003, p. 397). The researchers examined the three behaviors utilizing multiple regression analyses resulting in "significant amounts of variable in each third grade outcome, 35% for aggressive-disruptive behavior problems, 18% for academic performance, and 19% for social preference" (Flanagan, et al., 2003, p. 399). More males than females exhibited problem behaviors, and results utilizing Pearson's product moment correlation coefficient indicated "high levels of association among the three behaviors" (p. 399) characterized by 40% of the aggressive children who exhibited concomitant behaviors-hyperactivity-inattention and prosocial skill deficits; 24% of children showed elevated aggression without concomitant behaviors, and 30% of the children had no other difficulties. This case proved to be an effective strategy by utilizing multiple assessment tools in identifying high-risk aggressive children and supported Flanagan's et al. (2003) premise that aggression in children is usually associated with cognitive - social skill deficits or hyperactivity-inattention and that "children with any one of these problems appeared at increased risk for the other problems" (Flanagan, et al., 2005, p. 400).

Forbes, E., Shaw, D., Fox, N., Cohn, J., Silk, J., & Kovace, M. (2006). Maternal depression, child frontal asymmetry and child affective behavior as factors in child behavior problems. *Journal of Child Psychology and Psychiatry, 47*(1), 79-87.

Summary

The focus of this study was to determine to what extent affect regulation, frontal asymmetry, and childhood onset depression correlate with maternal depression. Participants consisted of 74 mother-child dyads drawn from a longitudinal study at the Western Psychiatric Institute and Clinic in Pittsburgh, Pennsylvania in which researchers examined behavior problems exhibited by children of parents diagnosed with depressive disorders. In this study, 44 out of the 74 mothers were diagnosed with depressive disorders characterized by "dysthymia before age 14 (n=39), or bipolar spectrum disorders before age 17 (n=5), (Forbes, et al., 2006, p. 81), and the remaining constituted the control group (n=30). The children ranged from ages three to nine, and they were examined in a psychophysiology lab, utilizing an electroencephalogram (EEG) to identify left or right frontal asymmetry. During subsequent visits, mother and child interactions were observed while the child performed affect tasks. Consistent with the authors' prediction and research findings in their literature review, the results of this study indicated that "maternal depression in combination with frontal asymmetry was related to children's behavior problems" (Forbes et al., 2006, p. 84). Also, high levels of aggression were associated with males from COD mothers. This study substantiated the role that maternal depression plays as an additional risk factor in the development of behavioral disorders and childhood aggression.

Analysis

According to Forbes et al. (2006), mothers with a history of depression sometimes have children who are "at increased risk for developing different forms of psychopathology" (p.79). Their study predicted that if the electroencephalograms and affect regulation behaviors of these children were examined, results would indicate high levels of aggression and adjustment problems associated with maternal depressive disorders. Forbes et al. (2006) divided 74 mother-child dyads into two groups; 44 were diagnosed with childhood onset depression (COD) during their youth and 30 who were free of COD that comprise the control group. Children ranging in ages from three to nine were selected because this developmental time frame was deemed important in examining affect regulation. Forbes et al. (2006) stated that "child affect regulation behavior was assessed on dimensions –such as negative affect, positive affect, and appropriate expression – critical to the development of behavior problems" (p. 80). Results from the electroencephalograms indicated COD mothers' children with left frontal asymmetry exhibited more anxious depressed problems, low affect regulation behavior, and "higher aggressive problems than the control group" (Forbes et al., 2006, p.84). In essence, Forbes et al. concluded that child behavior problems and aggression is associated with frontal asymmetry, affect regulation, and maternal depressive disorders. This study substantiated other research studies regarding childhood aggressions and its association with faulty regulation and maternal depressive disorders.

Grinberg, I., Dawkins, M., Dawkins, M., & Fullilove, C. (2005). Adolescents at risk for violence: An initial validation of the life challenges questionnaire and risk assessment index. *Adolescence, 40*(159), 573- 599.

Summary

The Life Challenges Questionnaire Teen Form is developed by clinical psychologists in Chicago at the Center of Applied Psychology and Forensic Studies. This form attempts to "help clinicians, educators, and parents identify children and adolescents who are coping poorly with the challenges of their lives and are at risk for involvement in violent behavior" {p. 576, ¶ 1). This research study was an attempt to validate the utility of their questionnaire by conducting a study consisting of 415 juvenile pre-trial detainees and 305 students from a Christian high school based in the Midwest. Embedded in this questionnaire was a Risk Assessment Index (RAI) consisting of 53 items directly correlated with risk factors identified prior research as predictors of youth violence. The paper and pencil version of the form was administered to participants in groups of 20. Questionnaire examined the following: family characteristics, peer relationships, community and school environment, and personality, behavioral, and psychological factors. Results indicated that the detainees scored higher on items relating to the assessment index that correlated with high levels of aggression than the Christian high school students, confirming the validity of the form as a viable assessment tool to identify students at risk for violence.

Analysis

This research study is based on the premise that assessment tools utilized to identify, predict, and measure youth at risk for committing violence are limited and that they fail to address relevant risk factors. According to the literature review provided by Grinberg et al. (2005), identifiable risk factors associated with childhood aggression and later youth violence, can essentially be grouped into four categories: "the family system, the school, personality and psychological factors, and the peer group" (p. 577). The Life-Challenges Questionnaire Teen Form by Grinberg et al. (2005) was designed to address these four areas, and this study was an attempt to validate its utility as a screening instrument to identify adolescents at high risk for committing violence. The questionnaire consisted of 120 items, 53 of which comprised the Risk Assessment Index (RAI) that was scattered within the assessment. The Risk Assessment Index had been documented to "reflect known correlates of youth violence" (p.584) and has a high reliability and validity coefficient. Study participants were randomly selected from a juvenile detention facility and a Christian-based high school, both located in the Midwest, ranging in ages 11 to 18. The final sample included 99 juvenile detainees, predominantly African-American students from low-income, single-family homes and 305 students of mixed ethnicity and mixed income levels. The pencil-paper version of the Life Challenges Questionnaire-Teen Form was administered to all participants in one sitting. Results from the two groups of adolescents differed remarkably in the areas of family, peer relationships, school environment, behavioral and psychological factors, which were consistent with the authors' hypotheses and validated by the chi square distribution. Multiple aggression analysis was applied to determine the impact of grade level, race, sex, and age on risk factors for violence and Cronbach's alpha scores measured validity in relation to internal consistency. All of the statistical data proved to be consistent with risk factors directly correlated with youth violence, indicating the Life Challenges Questionnaire-Teen Form to be a viable screening instrument for the early identification of youth at risk for violence. Data regarding high risk factors that predict youth violence is consistent with previous studies in my literature review.

Hodgins, S., Cree, A., Alderton, J., and Mak, T. (2008). From conduct disorders to severe mental illness: Associations with aggressive behaviour, crime and victimization. *Psychological Medicine, 38,* 975-987.

Summary

This article substantiated the life course persistent trajectory that is associated with early-onset aggression and posited that "conduct disorders in childhood or adolescence increases the likelihood of aggressive behaviour and violent crime in adulthood" (Hodgins, Cree, Alderton, & Max, 2008, p. 981). The study by Hodgins et al.(2008) linked conduct disorders with substance abuse, the development of schizophrenia, faulty parenting skills, and genetic loading. Hodgins et al. (2008) stated that "family studies have confirmed a genetic contribution to an early-onset stable pattern of antisocial behaviour...suggesting that these individuals inherit a vulnerability for CD as well as for schizophrenia (p.983). Study participants included 120 males and 85 females (n=205), from the urban areas of the United Kingdom with a median age of 38.5, previously diagnosed with severe mental illness characterized by "a principal diagnosis of schizophrenia, schizo-affective disorder, bipolar disorder, major depression, non-toxic psychosis" (Hodgins et al., 2008, p. 977).

All participants provided consent to obtain copies of their criminal and psychiatric records. Data indicated that 69 out of 135 patients diagnosed with conduct disorders prior to age 15 had "significantly higher rates of aggressive behaviour towards others, victimization, and criminal convictions than the patients without a childhood history of CD" (Hodgins, et al., 2008, p. 978). Results of the study confirm that a diagnosis of conduct disorder prior to age 15 suggested" long-term consequences for both men and women who subsequently develop severe mental illness" (Hodgins, et al., 2008, p. 981). Study results indicate the necessity for further research involving aggressive behavior and its association with mental illness and victimization in order to identify related causal factors.

Analysis

This research study conducted by Hodgins, Cree, Alderton, and Max (2008) is significant because it examined the relationship between children diagnosed with conduct disorders prior to age 15 and aggressive behavior as a predictor of violence later in adulthood, especially among adults with mental illness. Hodgins et al. (2008) posited that "conduct disorder is a precursor of persistent antisocial and aggressive behaviour and criminality" (p.982). Physical trauma in childhood was a major causal factor in the development of CD in children prior to age 15, which subsequently led to mental illness, usually schizophrenia (Hodges et al., 2008). Data from the participants (n=205) indicated that among men "42% fulfilled the criteria for CD prior to age 15 and the mean number of symptoms was 2.68 (S.D. = 3.09)" while women comprised "...22.4% with a mean number of symptoms 1.27 (S.D. =2.12)" (Hodgins et al., 2008, p.978). The authors suggested a genetic predisposition to CD and mental illness in children whose parents were diagnosed as carrying "the low activity allele of the genetic polymorphism encoding monoamine oxidase A" (Hodgins et al., 2008, p.984.) which was consistent with previous research by Moffitt et al.,(2004). Hodgins et al. (2008) further revealed that "parents who carry the susceptibility genes are more likely than parents without such genes to engage in behaviour such as physical maltreatment, maternal hostility, and smoking during pregnancy, that are known to contribute to the development of anti-social behaviour"(p. 984). Hodgins, et al. (2008) stated that certain home environments perpetuate aggressive behavior and "the prevalence rates of CD increases with the level of social deprivation" (p.984). Hodgins et al. (2008) posited that "children with CD enter adolescence and begin experiencing prodramal symptoms such as anxiety, they may lack even more than other adolescents developing psychosis, effective cognitive and behavioural coping skills" (p. 983). Well-adjusted parents in nurturing, positive environments are usually able to provide assistance to their adolescent children, but training programs are needed to teach parenting skills to those who are unable to address these problems to reduce the numbers of children-at-risk of developing CD.

Jaffe, S., Belsky, J., Harrington, H., Caspi, A., & Moffitt, T. (2006). When parents have a history of conduct disorder: How is the caregiving environment affected? *Journal of Abnormal Psychology, 115*(2), 309-319.

Summary

The purpose of this research study was to ascertain whether parents diagnosed with a history of conduct disorders could provide a warm, care giving environment for their children. Samples from this study originated from a third generation longitudinal study from the Dunedin Multidisciplinary Health and Development Study consisting of 2, 000 births form 1971 to 1973. The subjects were New Zealanders from various socio-economic backgrounds diagnosed with late onset conduct disorders during adolescence. At the time of the experiment, 22 was the average age of generation-2 parents, and 79% of the mothers and 99% of the fathers were residing with generation-3 children, which were now three years-of-age. Parents were videotaped at home interacting with their child and were paid for the study. Diagnostics and assessments had been administered by the health agency. Results indicated that parental age, intelligence, and socioeconomic status were factors directly associated with the quality of the home environment. Older parents with higher levels of intelligence had good, productive home environments. Low education levels, low income, and high unemployment were synonymous with poor environments characterized by harsh, inconsistent discipline, and partner violence.

Analysis

This was a third generation longitudinal study by Jaffe et al. (2005) based on the premise that "parents diagnosed with conduct disorder in adolescence experienced more socioeconomic disadvantage, more partner violence, and less positive romantic relationships than did parents who had no history of disorder, or parents who had a history of anxiety or depression" (p.311). Participants (n=246), designated as G2, who were now parents of children ranging in ages from three to five were selected and divided into groups characterized by the following: 1. parents diagnosed with a conduct disorder, but not exhibiting anxiety or depression (n=34), 2. parents diagnosed with anxiety or depressive disorders, but not conduct disorders (n=71), 3. parents diagnosed with both conduct disorder and anxiety or depressive disorders (n=46) and 4. Parents diagnosed as normal or having no disorders (n=78)), (Jaffe et al., 2006). Informative data was obtained from the G2 parents, utilizing a battery of inventories to examine the quality of life that they were providing for their children. The Braiker and Kelly (1999) four factor scale was administered to parents "residing with a partner 12 months prior to the researchers' home visit" (Jaffe et al., 2006) to examine interpersonal relationships. Partner violence was assessed utilizing the Conflict Tactic Scales (Strauss, 1990) and the Infant/Toddler Home Observation for Measurement of the Environment (HOME; Caldwell & Bradley, 1984) measured positive parenting skill levels or lack thereof, and parental involvement in maintaining a quality, supportive environment. Utilizing the no-disorder group as the reference category, researchers applied regression analysis, utilizing Stata's *xi* procedure to determine a correlation between conduct disorders, anxiety or depressive disorders, by comparison and contrast. Results (for the standard regression coefficients) indicated "no significant differences between G2 parents who had a history of conduct disorders without comorbid anxiety or depression" (Jaffee et al., 2006, p. 313). G2 parents diagnosed with any form of psychopathology exhibited less than optimal parenting skills than their peers; however, socio-economic status and older parents appeared to be the major indicators of whether parents, diagnosed with conduct disorders in their youth, could provide a quality home environment for a child. Jaffee et al. (2006) validated their hypotheses that "conduct disorder is unique among disorders of childhood and adolescence in its long term effects on more distal influences on children's development (e.g. domestic violence, socioeconomic disadvantage), but not on more proximal influences, such as specific parenting behaviors, or on child temperament" (p. 315). Jaffe et al. (2006) also indicated a direct correlation between early onset conduct problems, low intelligence, and neuropsychological deficits. Neurological deficits may interfere with one's ability to function in an educational or employment setting so early identification with the implementation of early intervention strategies could possibly avert youth misconduct.

Lier, P., & Crijnen, A. (2005). Trajectories of peer-nominated aggression: Risk status, predictors and outcomes. *Journal of Abnormal Child Psychology, 33* (1), 99-112.

Summary

The goal of Lier and Crijnen's (2005) study was to identify two developmental trajectories, early-onset aggression and normative-low aggression, by utilizing peer nominations as informants during one of the assessments. Lier and Crijnen (2005) posited that early onset aggression would be characterized by more physical aggression such as outcomes. *Journal of Abnormal Child Psychology, 33* (1), 99-112. According to the authors, "Attention deficit/hyperactivity (ADH) problems, oppositional defiant problems, and poor school functioning" (p. 101). Lier and Crijnen (2005) also suggested that gender distribution would be predominantly male. The sample for this study consisted of 287 randomly selected students from two inner cities of the Netherlands currently participating in a "school-based preventive intervention study targeting disruptive behavior in young children" (Lier & Crijnen, 2005, p.101). Peers in their classrooms nominated children three times during first, second, and third grades, utilizing four behavioral descriptions, and their classroom teachers rated participating students, utilizing the TRF/6-18 (Achenbach, 1991) behavior scale. During the study, collection of additional data resulted in the identification of another trajectory group, identified as moderate-persistent. Final results comparing all three trajectories indicated that children in the early-onset aggression trajectory were predominantly male and exhibited an increasing number of persistent conduct problems that led to more aggressive behaviors. These results validated Lier and Crijnen's (2005) hypothesis regarding childhood aggression as a major predictor of delinquency in adolescence, stating that "children who show antisocial behavior early in life ... will follow a life course persistent antisocial trajectory" (p. 99).

Analysis

Lier and Crijnen's (2005) comparative analysis of three developmental trajectories of childhood aggression utilized peer nominations as informants to increase the validity and reliability of their study. Lier and Crijnen (2005) suggested that peer nominations are "based on multiple informants and are therefore very reliable; they report about aggressive acts outside the presence of adults, and they reflect the social context in which children function" (p. 101). Lier and Crijnen (2005) criticized the methodology of previous research studies that relied solely on parental reporting in attempting to obtain data regarding childhood aggression, stating that "the semi-parametric group-based modeling approach used in many of these studies assumes equal variability in problematic behavior between identified classes" (p. 101). Lier and Crijnen (2005) also questioned the validity of these experiments stating that class is an important criterion because "more variability in classes with high-risk children than in classes with low risk children is anticipated" (p.101). During grades 1-3, the children were separated into groups of six, whereby they rated each other utilizing an assessment in which they identified classmates of either gender that fit four behavioral descriptions. Lier and Crijnen (2005) noted that "Cronbach's alpha results of this assessment ranged from .92 to.94 over the three assessments" (p. 102), indicating high internal consistency. Utilizing the TRF/6-18 (Achenbach, 1997), teachers identified the problem children in the group, and teacher ratings of children on a three-point scale resulted in .80, utilizing Cronbach's alpha. The Alabama Parenting Questionnaire (APQ; Shelton, Frick, & Wooton, 1996) was administered to parents during an at-home interview that consisted of 42 questions regarding their parenting skills, resulting in an average across four domains of .67 on Cronbach's alpha. Parental stress was also assessed utilizing the Nijmegen Parenting Stress Index (NPSI) resulting in a score of .88 utilizing Cronbach's alpha. In essence, the results indicated that children who have been diagnosed with early-onset aggression are at risk of continuing their aggressive behaviors throughout adolescence, especially if parental support is minimal. If the parents exhibit good parenting skills and are managing their stress levels, they are able to model behaviors that assist their children in self-regulation. This article supports other research that the researcher has obtained, and the documentation will be useful.

Linnet, K., Obel, C., Bonde, E., Thomsen, P., Secher, N., Wisborg, K., & Henriksen, T. (2006). Cigarette smoking during pregnancy and hyperactive-distractible preschooler's: A follow-up study. *Acta Pediatrica, 95,* 694-700.

Summary

The purpose of this study was to validate prior studies that suggest maternal smoking during the perinatal and prenatal periods of fetal development result in children whom later exhibit behavioral problems characterized by "hyperactivity and distractibility, hostile-aggressive, and anxious-fearful" (p. 694). According to the authors, "women who smoke 10 or more cigarettes per day during pregnancy had a 60% increased risk of having a child with hyperactive- distractible behavior" (p. 698). Participants (n=1355) were selected from a prenatal cohort within a longitudinal study conducted at Aarhus University's Hospital Department of Obstetrics in Denmark that initiated in 1989. Mothers completed questionnaires regarding their smoking habits at four weeks, eight weeks, and following the birth of their child. These women were grouped into three categories, based on how many cigarettes they smoked daily. Group I did not smoke at all; Group II smoked from one to nine cigarettes daily, and Group III smoked more than 10 cigarettes per day.

Statistical data pertaining to the births was obtained and documented by midwives. When the children were four years of age, the mothers were interviewed and completed questionnaires assessing their child's current behavior. Results indicated that maternal smoking during pregnancy is directly correlated with hyperactivity and distractibility in the offspring.

Analysis

According to Linet, Obel, Bonde, Thomsen, Secher, Wisborg, and Henriksen, (2006), "the physiological explanation for possible adverse effects of intrauterine exposures is that metabolites from tobacco smoke cross the placenta, and the fetus is exposed to 15% higher nicotine concentration than the smoking mother" (p. 694). High concentrations of nicotine exposure to an unborn fetus has been associated with "an increased risk of hostile-aggressive and anxious-fearful child behaviour" (Linet et al., 2006, p. 697). The authors distributed the Behar Preschool Behaviour Questionnaire questionnaires to the mothers, and the self-reporting data was consistent with other studies that determined that there is a link between maternal smoking during the prenatal period and behavior problems which manifest in young children at the pre-school level. This research study was based on the premise that cigarette smoking during the development of the fetus results in behavior problems characterized by hyperactivity and distractibility evidenced at three to five years of age. According to Linnet, Obel, Bonde, Secher, Thomeson, Wisborg, and Henriksen (2006), "the fetus is exposed to 15% higher nicotine concentration than the smoking mother as metabolites from tobacco smoke cross the placenta (p. 694).

Moffit, T. (2005). The new look of behavioral genetics in developmental
    psychopathology: Gene environment interplay in antisocial behaviors.
    Psychological Bulletin, 131(4), 553-554.

Summary

Moffitt sought to answer questions regarding the interplay between genes and environment in the development of childhood aggression by examining the role of familial influences characterized by bad parenting. In this article Moffitt (2005) declared that current research on childhood aggression and antisocial behavior is stuck on identifying bad parenting as a risk factor instead of a phenotype, and that to facilitate movement, new research assessment techniques need to focus on "behavioral-genetic designs, natural treatment studies, and randomized treatment experiments in order to inform strong etiological theory" (p.534). Moffitt completed an extensive and current review of the literature involving research studies that utilized thousands of twin pairs to determine whether its origin is genetic or environmental. Moffitt reviewed the major risk factors associated with childhood aggression such as maternal depression, maternal smoking, maternal rejection, poor parenting skills, and others, raising the question of genetic mediation. Moffitt concluded by describing behavioral genetics research strategies that she hopes will be implemented in the future.

Analysis

Moffitt has re-evaluated the way developmental psychology obtains information and has decided that researchers may need to take another direction, focusing on a genetic predisposition as a causal factor of childhood aggression and violence, instead of risk factors. Moffitt (2004) stated, "Without control for genetic variations, further risk-factor research remains ambiguous if not uninformative" (p. 534). According to Moffitt, when researching childhood aggression emphasis should focus on studying *rGE*, defined as "a passive correlation between genotype and on environmental measure" (p. 538) explaining that "a passive rGE confound occurs when a child's behavior and the environment his or her parents provide are correlated because they have the same origins in the parents' genotype" (p.538). Moffitt dispelled the importance that researchers place on the environment in the development of aggression and violence by examining research studies utilizing hundreds of identical twins raised in the same, quality environments and foster infants removed from criminal biological parents in adverse conditions and then placed in quality environments, suggesting that aggression and violence emerged due to deficiencies in the familial gene pool. Moffit (2005) revealed that only one gene, "the monoamine oxidase-A has been associated with aggressive behavior in humans when it is linked with a measurable environmental risk factor such as childhood maltreatment" (P. 545). Moffit indicated that gene research has a long way to go, and even though it is moving forward rapidly, it will require interdisciplinary cooperation of geneticists, psychologists, educators, and social scientists to isolate a gene and evaluate it without environmental influences. This article provides a wealth of current information that supports my research.

Tremblay, R., Nagin, D., Seguin, J., Zoccolillo, M., Zelazo, P., Boivin, M., et al. (2004). Physical aggression during early childhood: Trajectories and predictors. *Pediatrics,* 114(1), e43-e50.

Summary

The objective of Tremblay's et al. (2004) study was to identify trajectories of physical aggression within 17 to 42 months following infant births and to identify associated high-risk behaviors. The results indicate that the onset of physical aggression is approximately 17 months and that it escalates during the next three years. The high risk behavior declines after three years, depending on parenting skills and other risk factors. Tremblay also identified high risks factors that contribute to aggression in childhood. Tremblay et al.

(2004) believed that early intervention programs should be initiated at the pre-school level, between two and four years of age. This study modified the contextual parameters of early aggression research and initiated new benchmarks for investigating infants.

Analysis

The basic premise of this study is that a developmental trajectory would confirm physical aggression that manifests in adolescence and adulthood has its origins in infancy and toddlerhood. This three-year study at the Quebec Ministry of Health and Social Sciences, consisting of a stratified random sample (based on infant's gender and mother's geographical residence near the clinic) of 504 single births, sought to identify the onset of aggression behavior in infants and to examine other concomitant high risk behaviors.

Initial interviews were conducted with parents and infants at 5 months to obtain information regarding infants' current temperament and mothers' skill levels of parenting.

Additional information regarding parents' anti-social behaviors exhibited during their high school years was obtained because Tremblay et al. (2004) determined that parents with a history of discipline problems in high school (i.e. verbal abuse, suspensions for fighting) "usually are at highest risk of not learning to regulate physical aggression in early childhood" (p.43). This is critical, according to social learning theorists, because children can not model what they have not seen. Subsequent data was collected from mothers at 17 and 30 and from both parents at 42 months after birth to assess their levels of physical aggression, utilizing items from rating scales validated in other longitudinal studies.

Results of the developmental trajectory indicated that 14% of the children followed a rising level of physical aggression and 28% exhibiting little or no physical aggression, while the majority 58% exhibited modest aggression levels. Concomitant risk factors such as maternal smoking, drinking and depression during the perinatal period of the infants, along with low educational levels and poverty, were associated with toddlers in the high physical aggression group. Another associated risk factor was the presence of siblings in the high physical aggression group because they were utilized as targets. This study substantiated data that physical aggression is evidenced in infancy and early childhood, making the case those intervention strategies should be initiated at birth to three years of age.

Tremblay, R. (2004). Decade of behavior distinguished lecture: Development of physical aggression during infancy. *Infant Mental Health Journal, 25(5)*, 399-407.

Summary

Tremblay analyzed longitudinal studies from New Zealand, Canada, and the United States, challenging prior research related to the onset of physical aggression in school-aged children. Tremblay provided a brief historical analysis of the age-crime curve devised by the Belgian statistician Adolfe Quetelet in the 1800s that has been the foundation of misinformation for decades regarding the onset of aggressive criminal behaviors. Tremblay utilized this information to explain why previous research studies on aggression began with the study of adolescents. Tremblay cited biological and environmental risks factors that contribute to aggression during an infant's perinatal period, including the maternal educational level and maternal smoking, indicating that early intervention prior to students entering kindergarten is the best strategy to minimize physical and negative aggressive behaviors.

Analysis

Tremblay's theoretical framework appears to be based on the philosophical underpinnings of Aristotle in that he believes to fully understand the outcome of anything, a person must return to its origin. Tremblay states that "if we aim to understand the development of a phenomenon, it is wise to start looking before the phenomenon becomes apparent" (p.402) Tremblay's ideology provides a rationale into his research regarding the onset of aggression and explains why he disregarded Quetelet's age-crime curve devised in 1880 which was antiquated and why he established adolescence as the stage in which aggressive behaviors escalated, but not designating when or how aggression develops. However, Tremblay outlined the developmental origins of aggression, focusing on gene-environment interactions. According to Tremblay, aggression is evidenced in infants as early as four months of age and peaks at 24-42 months. Whether it escalates further is interdependent on the child's genetic predisposition and the quality of the child's environment. Tremblay cited studies utilizing children who were misused in childhood, but who had inherited "a functional polymer in the gene coding for the neurotransmitter metabolizing enzyme monoamine oxydose A (MAOA) and who were at less risk of exhibiting serious antisocial behavior" (p. 405) indicating the power of genetic predisposition. Additional information provided by Tremblay pertaining to the onset of aggression research from other studies around the world substantiate high risks factors associated with aggression such as the maternal educational level, maternal smoking and improper nutrition during the perinatal period. Tremblay also completed an item analysis explaining specific characteristics of infants' aggressive behaviors (i.e. infant pushes others to get what he/she wants) exhibited at various stages of development. Tremblay referenced Aristotle, Rousseau, Hobbes, and other philosophers to give credence to the idea that a child is a product of his or her environment and that he/she must control primitive instincts to successfully integrate into society. If these instincts are not self-regulated, then parents and other adults must provide the training. This article is an excellent addition to my bibliography in that it encompasses the major points of the depth section of this paper.

Literature Review Essay

Acts of violence perpetrated by youth is a global affair that has reached unprecedented numbers. Incidents of youth violence permeate the mass media across continents from Europe to Asia, identifying youth violence as a major societal problem of the 21st century (Moffitt, 2005; Tremblay, Nagin, Seguin, Zoccolillo, Zelano, Boivon, et al. 2004). These violent youth have changed the landscape of the environment and now dictate the manner in which individuals socially interact within communities. According to statistical data compiled by Grinberg, Dawkins, Dawkins, and Fullilove (2005), youth violence is characterized by "gang violence, teen-on-teen homicide, and domestic battery involving children and adolescents, and aggravated sexual assault have raised concern among policymakers, law enforcement officials, school administrators and others" (p. 574). Senior citizens barricade themselves in gated communities, afraid to venture outside after dusk because "10% of the families in any community account for more than 50% of those communities criminal offenses" (Moffitt, 2005, p.533, ¶2). Participation in indoor, structured, activities has replaced outdoor, physical play for children, because parents, fearing for their safety, restrict children's mobility in parks and other public places where older youth gather. This has resulted in increased sedentary time for children who play video games and watch television that in turn facilitates health issues that contribute to obesity (Pugliese, Tinsley, 2007). Youth violence also affects the workplace, and health care professionals, especially nurses, are searching for safer places of employment (Dragon, 2006). According to statistics, hospital nurses, more than any other occupation, are experiencing workplace violence worldwide (Dragon, 2006). Schools have also become inundated with violent youth who threaten the educational process on a daily basis. Maintaining a safe environment conducive to learning has become more of a priority in educational institutions around the world. Grinberg, et al. (2005) reported that "the majority of violent juvenile crime peaks during the after school hours between 3 p.m. and 5 p.m. on school days and in the evenings between 8 p.m. and 10 p.m. on non-school days" (p. 574). Males between the ages of 15 to 17 often commit these crimes (Grinberg, Dawkins, Dawkins, & Fullilove, 2005; Feder, Levant, and Dean, 2007). The reason for this statistic is that, according to Feder, Levant, and Dean (2007), "clinical and empirical research conducted over the past two decades has suggested that the socialization of boys to conform to traditional notions of masculinity such as toughness, aggression, dominance, and the restriction of emotional suppression may heighten the potential for boys to engage in violence" (p. 387). They suggest that boys are socialized into aggression and violence, facilitated by the media, parents, peer groups, and easy access to firearms. This socialization process is costly, and Grinberg, Dawkins, Dawkins, & Fullilove, (2005) " estimate that the high school dropout, the heavy drug abuser, and the career criminal costs society 3 million dollars annually in legal, psychological services, lost wages, and justice system costs" (p.573). In essence, the problem of youth violence has become deleterious, and researchers are now stressing the necessity of early identification of high risk factors that contribute to aggressive behaviors leading to violence (Alink, Mesman, Zeijl, Stolk, Koot, & Juffer, 2006). Flanagan, Bierman, and chi-Ming Kam (2003) argued that early intervention is "most effective if it is highly selective, focusing only on those children with two or three problems who appear to be at highest risk for later problems" (p. 307). Prior to identifying these children, researchers must obtain some basic understanding of underlying factors that contribute to the etiology of aggressive, violent, behavior in order to facilitate the development of appropriate risk assessments and formulate strategies. Concerned professionals must engage in intervention strategies that will minimize, if not alleviate, these problems exhibited by youth in schools, the workplace, and communities that characterize our lives with fear and intimidation, resulting in an inability to thrive.

Therefore, this depth essay will explore current research studies that examine the onset of aggression and risk factors that contribute to violent and aggressive behaviors in youth exhibited prenatally to adolescence. The essay also will identify correlates of violent behaviors that are specific to school settings. In addition, the conclusion to this essay will examine the gaps and deficiencies in this literature review.

Developmental Pathways of Aggression and Violence

Researchers have now identified two distinct developmental pathways of youth aggression and violence, classifying the development of aggression into early-onset persistent type and late-onset adolescent type. The early-onset persistent type was originally defined by Moffitt (2001, 2005) and was characterized by early signs of aggressive behavior evidenced as early as 36 months and continuing throughout childhood, adolescence, and adulthood. Causal factors were identified as fetal brain damage resulting from prenatal and postnatal complications, coupled with an adverse familial environment, poverty, and low educational levels (Hodges et al., 2008; Moffitt, 2005; and Tremblay, 2005). During this time frame, Garbino (2008) suggested that "two principal processes that control the developmental pathway for aggression in childhood are the ideas a child learns about aggression (cognitive structuring) and the experiences a child has in situations where aggressive behavior is modeled and reinforced (behavioral rehearsal)" (p.2). He further stated that children who are at risk of continuing aggression into adolescence are those who have been characterized as "impulsive, emotionally insensitive, having a high activity level, being of less-than average intelligence, and being relatively fearless" (p. 2). Lier and Crijnen (2005) also cited other concomitant behaviors such as "attention deficit hyperactivity (ADH) problems, oppositional defiant problems, and poor school functioning"(p.101) that contribute to aggression into adolescence.

The second developmental pathway involves late-onset aggression when adolescent youth are involved with undesirable peer groups who participate in aggressive and violent acts (Feder, Levant, & Dean (2007). Participants of the late- aggression type do not exhibit aggressive behaviors until middle or late adolescent (Brennan et al. 2003). According to Brennan (2003) "the prognosis for this group is somewhat more promising than for the early-onset group because late starters usually desist from antisocial behavior by their early twenties" (p. 309). Albeit, researchers agree that early identification of infants and children exhibiting these behaviors is critical to reducing violence and aggressive behaviors in our youth (Anhalt, Telzrow, Brown, 2007; Flanagan, Bierman, & Chi-Ming, 2003; Alink, Mesman, Zeijl, Stolk, Koot, & Juffer, 2006).

Onset of Aggression

Onset of aggression is defined as, "harm done with malevolent intent" and "those acts that inflict bodily or mental harm on others" (Tremblay, 2005, p. 108). The etiology of aggressive behavior is a contentious issue based on the nature versus nurture dichotomy, which has been debated for decades. From these two schools of thought emerged the theoretical framework of Bandura's social learning theory, Vygotsky's socio-historical theory, Piaget's theory of cognitive development, and recently Tremblay's research based theory regarding the innate, biological origins of aggression. Bandura (1977, 2004) maintained that human behavior is not innate and that aggression, like all behaviors, is imitated, learned and shaped by environmental stimuli. Vygotsky's theory also maintained that behavior is learned within an environmental context in which children's physical and psychological activities are adult directed. Piaget utilized a biological approach to child growth and development, focusing on cognition that begins in infancy, based on a few innate reflexes. However, Tremblay (2005) asserted that all physically aggressive behaviors are innate, developmental, and evidenced in infancy. Tremblay's theoretical framework appears to be based on the philosophical underpinnings of Aristotle in that to fully understand the outcome of anything, a person must return to its origin. Tremblay stated that "if we aim to understand the development of a phenomenon, it is wise to start looking before the phenomenon becomes apparent" (p.402). Tremblay's ideology provides a rationale into his research regarding the onset of aggression and explains why he disregarded Quetelet's age-crime curve devised in 1880 that was considered obsolete and established adolescence as the stage in which aggressive behaviors escalate. However, Tremblay did not designate when or how aggression develops.

Studies identifying the onset of aggression in infancy have been few until recently, due to the fact that data collection has been limited to pre-school and primary students who exhibit high risk aggressive behaviors. This rationale justifies why Bandura and other researchers emphasized aggressive behavior as learned through imitation and reinforcement in that their studies relied on data collected in the later stages of a child's development. However, current studies indicate that aggressive behaviors are developmental, and the onsets of these behaviors are visible in violent youth during infancy and early childhood (Tremblay et al., 2004; Alink, Mesman, Zeijl, Stolk, Juffer, Koot, Kranenburg, & Jzendoorn, 2006). Tremblay outlined the developmental origins of gene-environment interactions that facilitate aggression, focusing on the early-onset persistent type of aggressive behaviors and associated risk factors. According to Tremblay, aggression is evidenced in infants as early as four months of age and peaks at 24-42 months (p.403). He also suggested that whether it escalates further is interdependent of the child's genetic predisposition and the quality of the child's environment (Tremblay, 2004). Current studies initiated at birth concur with Tremblay's findings, identifying the onset of aggression in infancy and now provide relevant data indicating that aggressive behaviors are evidenced in infants as early as five months and peak at 42 months (Tremblay, Nagin, Seguin, Zoccolillo, Zelazo, Boivin, Percusse, & Japel, 2004); Tremblay, 2004; Moffitt, 2005; Flanagan, Bierman, & Kam, 2003).

Tremblay et al. (2004) were among the first researchers to utilize a developmental trajectory to assess physical aggression in infants and to identify risk factors that would predict infants with high levels of aggression. A random population sample of 504 families with five-month old newborns participated in the longitudinal three-year study at the Quebec Ministry of Health and Social Sciences. Following the initial interview at five months, mothers were interviewed at 17, 30, and 42 months after the birth of their child. In this study, 58% of the infants exhibited modest aggression, 28% displayed little or no physical aggression, and 14% exhibited high physical aggression. Alink, Mesman, Zeijl, Stolk, Juffer. Koot, Kranenburg, and Ijzendoorn (2006) duplicated Tremblay's 2004 study, continuing to examine aggressive physical behavior in 10 to 50 month-old children utilizing a developmental trajectory of 12, 24, and 36 months. They modified the experimental design, utilizing more testing instruments with additional items, and interviewing both parents to obtain data. Tremblay interviewed the father at the initial and final meetings only. Participants were administered the Screening and Intervention of Problem Behavior in Toddlerhood (SCRIPT) and the Physical Aggression Scale for Early Childhood (PASEC). Their findings were consistent with Tremblay et al. (2004) in that aggression levels increased at 24 to 36 months and that (males were higher than female levels), declining after 36 months. Alink et al. (2006) attributed the decline of aggression after 36 months due to children regulating their own behaviors and the rise of aggression to the emergence of anger and frustration evidenced after 12 months of age. Both studies concluded that physical aggression is present in early-onset infants during the first year of life, and concomitant risk factors such as maternal smoking, drinking, depression during the perinatal period of the infants, along with low educational levels and poverty, were associated with toddlers in the high physical aggression group.

Risk Factors that Contribute to Aggression

Prior to the first year of life, associated prenatal and perinatal risk factors may contribute to the development of aggressive behaviors (Brennan, Hall, Bor, Najman, & Williams, 2003; Moffitt, 2005). The prenatal period extends from conception to birth, and the perinatal period is the timeframe encompassing the fifth month of pregnancy to the first month after the child is born. The most important task immediately following conception during the third and eighth week is the development of brain cells and their migration throughout the central nervous system (Tremblay, 2005). This is a critical period of development for the fetus because normal development can be arrested by internal and external environmental influences. These influences are known as risk factors. Moffit (2005) defined a risk factor as a variable, "if it has a documented predictive relation with antisocial outcomes, whether or not it is causal" (p. 534) and identifies maternal depression, maternal smoking, maternal rejection, and poor parenting skills as major risk factors associated with childhood aggression. Tremblay et al. (2004) also identified risk factors from studies all over the world evidenced during the prenatal and perinatal period that have an "adverse effect on the structural or functional components of the central nervous system" (p.161) and cited them as predictors of high aggression. The five highest correlates of aggression of both researchers are maternal depression, maternal and familial antisocial behavior, and the socio-economic status of the mother, maternal smoking, and maternal use of illicit drugs during pregnancy.

    Maternal depression and stress during the prenatal and perinatal periods have been associated with aggression and adverse problems in childhood (Tremblay, 2000; Anhalt, Telzrow, & Brown, 2007; Moffit, 2001, 2004). Maternal depression is identified as a major risk factor in "that psychopathology symptoms during pregnancy have physiological consequences for the fetus" (Bonari, Pinto, Ahn, Einarson, Steiner, & Koren, 2004, p. 730). Maternal depression and stress during the prenatal and perinatal periods have been linked to preeclampsia and neonatal retardation and have been linked to problems in fetal brain development affecting the neurological development of the fetus (Bonari et al., 2004). Findings suggest that its effects during the pre-natal and peri-natal periods are time specific and may be irreversible (Bonari, et. al, 2004; Anhalt et al. 2007). According to Anhalt et al. (2007), "the peri-natal programming hypothesis argues that exposures during critical periods of fetal development alter the physiological environment in a manner that programs offspring to display specific disorders or conditions, despite the reversal of these negative exposures later in the developmental period" (p.84). The authors also suggested that "increased levels of maternal anxiety and depression during the second and third trimesters predicted poor neonatal adaptation and poor health" (p.77). Women exhibiting high levels of depression during the first trimester produce infants with neuropsychological deficits associated with schizophrenia that manifests itself during adolescence (Anhalt et al., 2007; Arsenault, Tremblay, Boulerice, & Saucier, 2003). Anhalt et al. (2007) also cited a study conducted by Huizink, Mulder, & Buitelaar (2004) in which the authors posited that maternal stress results in a "cascade of hormonal and neurochemical responses to stress that adversely and permanently alters fetal central nervous system development, contributing to later psychological and behavioral outcomes" (p. 76). This study resulted in significant support for the correlation of maternal stress during the perinatal period with potential developmental problems in children in the first grade, especially when other socioeconomic factors are considered. According to Anhalt, et al. (2007), maternal stress is associated with depressive disorders and aggression in children. The authors indicated that "20% of randomly screened pregnant women met clinical criteria for depression" (Anhalt et al., 2007, p.85), suggesting that the numbers are probably twice as high in women from impoverished environments. Anhalt et al. (2007) postulated that during the prenatal and perinatal stages of development, depressed mothers produce "hormonal and neurochemical responses to stress, adversely and permanently altering fetal central nervous system development, mothers were randomly sampled during a prenatal check-up, and they agreed to full psychiatric assessments during the initial interviews. Due to various reasons, data was collected from 132 mothers at the following benchmarks: 14 and 36 weeks prenatal, 3 and

12 months postpartum, and at age 11 for each child. The children were evaluated at age 11 to determine whether cognitive development could play a role in mediating aggressive and violent behaviors. Various assessment tools were utilized to measure the children's expression of anger and cognitive abilities (i.e. CAPA which is a psychiatric interview for children and the WISC-III Wechsler Intelligence Scale). The study was extensive, exploring additional family characteristics including the biological father's criminal activity and anti-social personality disorders. Findings indicated that the time frame during which maternal depression occurs is significant and dictates the types of behavior problems that occur later in childhood. A higher incidence of violence and aggressive behaviors were noted in children whose mothers were depressed three months postpartum than other children. Boys were more likely to commit violent and/or aggressive acts than girls, and overall, these children exhibited anger, attention, and cognitive problems. In essence, maternal depression results in a wide range of adverse behaviors during the perinatal and post-partum periods.

Depression prior to birth increases the risk of more depression after pregnancy, and when mothers, the primary care givers, are unable to function in that capacity and are not responsive to an infant's needs, the infant suffers, resulting in neglect. Concomitant behaviors associated with neglect follow these mothers, facilitating developme problems in their children. Bonari et al., (2004) stated that "studies have found that mental illness can affect a mother's functional status, her ability to obtain prenatal care and her ability to avoid unhealthy behavior. Women suffering from depression are more likely to smoke or use alcohol or other which may confound pregnancy outcomes (p. 731).

Bonari et al. (2004) conducted an extensive review of the literature regarding the affects of untreated maternal depression during pregnancy, specifically during the perinatal period revealing that depression facilitates psychopathology in their offspring along with concomitant physical problems. According to Bonari et al. (2004), "1 in 5 pregnant women experience depression but few seek treatment" (p. 727) and "50% to 60% continue to suffer from depression in the postpartum period" (p. 731). This is serious because postpartum depression may account for "30,000 to 35,000 suicides yearly in North America" (Bonari et al., 2004, p. 727). Maternal depression is also correlated with developmental delays in their infants, especially when mothers exhibit postpartum depression. Bonari et al. (2004) suggested that, "studies have found that these children are 6 times more likely to develop depression than are children of mothers without depression, suggesting that genetic susceptibility has a role, in addition to environment" (p.733). The research also addressed the impact of maternal stress on the unborn fetus caused by the hypothalmo-pituitary-adrenal axis (HPA). Hyperactivity of the hypothalmo-pituitary-adrenal (HPA) axis, stimulated by stress, is characterized by preterm deliveries, low birth weight, spontaneous abortion, and other poor fetal outcomes due to hormones that cross the placenta stimulating neurotoxins during critical periods of fetal programming. Bonari et al. (2004) claimed that "the biological deregulation that occurs in depression may not be ideal for pregnancy" (p. 733) and that the emotional status of pregnant women needs to be monitored as closely as their physical status within obstetrics during this critical time period.

Maternal cigarette smoking during pregnancy is another high risk factor associated with childhood aggression and other developmental delays (Brook, Zhang, Rosenberg, & Brooks, 2006; Tremblay, 2004). Nicotine is the drug in tobacco that causes addiction, and the carbon monoxide along with eleven other gases it contains has been linked to cardio vascular diseases, low birth weight, stillborn and premature infants (Griffths, Wooley, Avasarala, & Weiner, 2005; Melvin & Gaffney, 2004, Linnet, Obel, Bonde, Hove, Wisborg, & Brink, 2006). In a longitudinal study conducted by Linnet et al. (2006), 1355 pregnant Danish women were administered questionnaires during their second and third trimesters to ascertain information regarding their smoking habits. Three years later, these women were interviewed and completed another self-administered questionnaire regarding their children's behavior. The children of mothers who smoked in excess of 10 cigarettes per day were found to have "a 60% increased risk of hyperactivity and distractibility perceived by the parents" (p.694). The nicotine in cigarettes leads to a 40% decrease in oxygen that is a major causal factor of hyperactivity. Linnet et al. (2006) suggested that prenatal exposure to smoking is also linked to conduct disorders in children.

In another longitudinal study conducted by Monuteaux, Blacker, Biederman, Fitzmzurice, and Buka (2006), prenatal exposure to smoking was linked to conduct disorders in children. In this study, 928 subjects were taken from twelve medical schools across the United States to participate in the National Collaborative Perinatal Project; 692 infants and their mothers were followed from pregnancy to age 22 and consistent with other studies, maternal smoking during pregnancy appears to be associated with behavior problems.

Another major risk factor associated with aggressive behaviors are familial influences characterized by prior family criminal behavior, maternal rejection, lack of parental supervision or involvement, child abuse, and poor overall parenting practices (Tremblay, 2004). Feder, Levant, and Dean (2007) suggested that parental influence is the major determinant of whether children develop aggressive and violent behaviors because they influence every aspect of a child's immediate environment. Jaffe, Belsky, Harrington, Caspi, and Moffitt (2006) conducted a longitudinal study to examine whether parents diagnosed with a history of conduct disorder could provide a warm, caregiving environment for their children. The subjects were New Zealanders from various socio-economic backgrounds who had been diagnosed with late onset conduct disorders during adolescence. Participants (n=246), designated as G2, who were now parents of children ranging in ages three to five, were selected and divided into four groups characterized by the following: (1) parents diagnosed with a conduct disorder, but not exhibiting anxiety or depression (n=34), (2) parents diagnosed with anxiety or depressive disorders, but not conduct disorders (n=71), (3) parents diagnosed with both conduct disorder and anxiety or depressive disorders (n=46), and (4) parents diagnosed as normal and having no disorders (n=78)) (Jaffe et al., 2006). Informative data was obtained from the G2 parents utilizing a battery of inventories to examine the quality of life they were providing for their children. The Braiker and Kelly (1999) four factor scale was administered to parents "residing with a partner 12 months prior to the researchers' home visit" (Jaffe et al., 2006) to examine interpersonal relationships. Partner violence was assessed utilizing the Conflict Tactic Scales (Strauss, 1990), and the Infant/Toddler Home Observation for Measurement of the Environment (Caldwell & Bradley, 1984) measured positive parenting skill levels or lack thereof, and parental involvement in maintaining a quality, supportive environment. Utilizing the no-disorder group as the reference category, researchers applied regression analysis utilizing Stata's *xi* procedure to determine a correlation between conduct disorders, anxiety or depressive disorders, by comparison and contrast. Results for the standard regression coefficients indicated "no significant differences between G2 parents who had a history of conduct disorders without co morbid anxiety or depression" (Jaffee et al., 2006, p. 313). G2 parents diagnosed with any form of psychopathology exhibited less than optimal parenting skills than their peers; however, socio-economic status and older parents appeared to be the major indicators of whether parents, diagnosed with conduct disorders in their youth, could provide a quality home environment for a child (Jaffee et al., 2006).

At the time of the experiment, 22 was the average age of generation-2 parents, and 79% of the mothers and 99% of the fathers were residing with generation-3 children, which were now three years old. Parents were videotaped at home interacting with their child and were paid for the study. Diagnostics and assessments had been administered by the health agency. Results indicated parental age, intelligence, and socioeconomic status were factors directly associated with the quality of the home environment. Older parents with higher levels of intelligence had good, productive home environments. Low education levels, low income, and high unemployment were synonymous with poor environments characterized by harsh, inconsistent discipline, and partner violence. Thus, parents who have a history of conduct disorders, living in an impoverished environment, with low incomes and high unemployment are at higher risks for modeling adverse behavior, resulting in children, especially boys, who may exhibit various levels of aggression and violence. This social constructionist ideology also forms the premise of one of the authors (Levant, 2007) whose theory of normative male alexithymia he described as "the inability to put emotions into words" (Feder, Levant, & Dean, 2007, p. 390). Levant's research revealed that, during the initial stages of child development, boys equal or surpasses girls in emotional and physical expression of their emotions. However, by age six, parents and peers alter the language acquisition skills of boys (i.e. via shaping) "leading boys to suppress, channel, and tune out their vulnerable emotions" (Feder, Levant, & Dean, 2007, p. 391). Feder et al.'s (2007) research further examined how boys are taught not to display tears or fears, but are encouraged to exhibit aggression, suggesting this is another prelude to male violence. The authors noted that "these results of gender role socialization predisposes boys to engage in violence" (Feder, Levant, & Dean, 2007, p.391), which provides justification for a higher incidence of violence associated with males.

Maternal educational level is directly correlated with all of the risk factors associated with childhood aggression and violence (Griffiths, Woolley, Avasarala, & Wiener, 2005; Tremblay, 2004). Mothers who give birth before the age of 18 and do not complete high school are more prone than mothers with higher educational levels to have children in the high risk aggressive group (Griffiths et al. 2005). This is due mainly to a lack of knowledge regarding pre-natal and post natal birth effects and poor parenting skills during the child's development. In a study assessing maternal parenting skills, researchers observed maternal coercive practices with five year-olds during role playing, hypothesizing that under pressure, mothers with aggressive boys exhibited limited "cognitive response repertoires to child noncompliance" (Beauchaine et al., 2002, p.91). Mothers of aggressive children aid in their children's negative behaviors by not providing them with alternate solutions, so as the children develop, they are unable to apply self-regulatory strategies because they have not acquired any. Additional research indicates that uneducated mothers with young children are more likely to suffer from depression than any other group due to their low socioeconomic status and the psychological strain of rearing an infant without emotional and financial support (Flanagan, et al., 2003; Hester, et al., 2003; Lenneke, et al., 2006).

Other risk factors involve prenatal, perinatal, and postnatal obstetrical complications. These include preeclampsia, umbilical cord prolepses, fetal distress, hypoxia, chemical substances in the body, anatomical brain anomalies, and other associated complications. In a study conducted by Arseneault et al. (2002) to determine whether these complications predicted aggression and violence in children and adolescents, information was collected from the medical records of 831 low-socioeconomic French Canadian boys participating in an ongoing longitudinal study. Behavior files for these students span kindergarten to adolescence. These boys had been rated by their teachers at age six to determine levels of aggression, and at age 17, they were asked to rate their own behaviors at home and school. The researchers utilized the data from these two benchmarks to create an obstetrical complication scale. The results of the scale indicated that among all obstetrical complications, the highest correlation with physical aggression and violence was preclampsia. Preclampsia is characterized by high blood pressure during pregnancy, resulting in concomitant problems such as fetal distress in which labor has to be induced to save the life of the fetus (Arseneault et al., 2002). The data also indicated that despite obstetrical complications, throughout the development of a child, the familial environment plays a major role in determining whether the child will learn to control and manage his or her aggressive behavior.

Whether risk factors are environmental, behavioral, or genetic, probable or established, they are indicators associated with a larger problem that affects one's quality of life. In the case of youth aggression and violence, they are indicators that should no longer be ignored and should act as screening mechanisms for students who have already been identified as aggressive and potentially violent.

Biological Predictors of Aggression

Even though a specific gene has not been identified to suggest a genetic predisposition towards aggression and violence, Moffitt (2005) stated that people should not assume that environment is the cause of every aggressive behavior, because evidence supports the validity of biological predictors. Moffitt (2005) re-evaluated the way developmental psychology obtains information, and he has decided that researchers may need to take another direction, focusing on a genetic predisposition as a causal factor of childhood aggression and violence, instead of risk factors. Moffitt (2005) stated that "without control for genetic variations, further risk-factor research remains ambiguous if not uninformative" (p. 534). According to Moffitt, when researching childhood aggression, emphasis should focus on studying *rGE*, defined as "a passive correlation between genotype and on environmental measure" (p. 538). He also explained that "a passive rGE confound occurs when a child's behavior and the environment his or her parents provide are correlated because they have the same origins in the parents' genotype" (p.538.¶ 1). Moffitt dispelled the importance that researchers place on the environment in the development of aggression and violence by examining research studies utilizing hundreds of identical twins raised in the same, quality environments and foster infants removed from criminal biological parents in adverse conditions who were placed in quality environments, suggesting that aggression and violence emerge due to deficiencies in the familial gene pool. Moffit (2005) revealed that only one gene, "the monoamine oxidase-A has been associated with aggressive behavior in humans when it is linked with a measurable environmental risk factor such as childhood maltreatment" (p. 545). She indicated that gene research has a long way to go, and even though this research is moving forward rapidly, it will require the interdisciplinary cooperation of geneticists, psychologists, educators, and social scientists to isolate a gene and evaluate it without environmental influences.

However, according to Retz, Retz-Junginger, Supprian, Thorne, and Rosler, (2004), that time has arrived because they have found that aggression and violence are directly associated with "serotonergic genes" (p. 416). Retz et al. (2004) suggested "a possible relation between the 5-HT transporter promoter gene polymorphism and violence" (p.417). In a study conducted in Germany at the Forensic-Psychiatric Institute of the University of Saarland Homburg, participants consisting of 153 male volunteers ranging from ages 16 to 70 years were divided into two groups, violent and non-violent. Violence was defined as "overt and intentional physically aggressive behavior against another person" (Retz et al., 2004, p. 417). The violent groups' offenses were characterized by physical injury, homicide, and sexual assaults, while the non-violent groups were characterized by traffic violations and fraud. All participants were administered neurological and psychological evaluations followed by genotyping utilizing their specific blood samples. The Eysenck Impulsive Questionnaire (EIC) was administered to assess levels of impulsiveness (Eysenck, Daum, Schugens, & Diehl, 1990), and the Wender Utah Rating Scale (WURS-K) was administered to identify symptoms associated with attention deficit hyperactive disorder (Wender, 1995). Genotyping involved DNA amplification to visualize the long and short alleles of the gene. The authors utilized the SPSS for windows to correlate statistical data between genotypes, the EIC, and the WURS-K. Results indicated a "significant association between the 5-HT transporter gene polymorphism and violent behavior" (Retz et al., 2004, p. 421).

A review of the literature also associates low levels of serotonin and cerebrospinal fluid with violent offenders (Beaver, DeLisi, Wright, and Vaugnh, 2009; Retz, et al., 2004; Davidson, Putman, & Lee & Coccaro, 2001; Larson, 2000). It appears that low levels of cerebrospinal fluid, decreased levels of serotonin, and concentrations of 5-hydroxyindolacetic acid facilitate a short circuit in the neural circuitry of the brain, stimulate aggression, and are associated with violence (Beaver et al., 2009). Serotonin is a neurotransmitter that is released into the synapse space that separates adjacent nerve cells. These nerve cells bind with receptors to inhibit or stimulate activity within the brain regulating various physical and mental functions. Therefore, it is not surprising that the prefrontal cortex that has been directly linked to aggression and violence would contain more serotonin receptors than any other part of the human brain. Additional current research conducted by Beaver et al. (2009) substantiated these biological predictors of aggression, arguing that "genetic factors have a direct effect on youthful misconduct" (p. 147).

Overall, the finding of this literature review tends to associate a strong genetic link with adolescent aggression, delinquency, and violence. However, since there is a need for more research, biological predictors should never be considered in isolation without considering environmental influences. Both should be viewed as an integrated entity when evaluating the etiology of aggression and violence.

Correlates of Violent Behaviors in School Settings

Until recently, violence in schools was characterized by the occasional altercation between two students in the corridors between classes, initiated by the school bully. The altercation was brief, lasting only minutes, because instructors would intervene separating the participants. Currently, violence within schools is so widespread that Indicators of School Crime and Safety #6 (2007) provided the following data: "78 percent of schools experience one or more violent incidents of crime, 17 percent experience one or more serious violent incidents, 46 percent experience one or more thefts, and 68 percent experience another type of crime" (p.1). The publication titled *Indicators of School Crime and Safety* (2007) also utilized the following definitions for the *categories*:

> *Serious violent incidents* include rape or attempted rape, sexual battery other than rape, physical attack or fight with a weapon, threat of physical attack with a weapon, and robbery with or without a weapon.
>
> *Violent incidents* include serious violent incidents plus physical attacks or fights without a weapon, threats of physical attacks without a weapon.
>
> *Other incidents* include possession of a firearm or explosive device, possession of a knife or sharp object, distribution, possession or use of illegal drugs or alcohol, and vandalism. (p.6)

Given the current statistical data, violence in schools imitates violence on the streets, in communities, and in society in general. Schools are supposed to be safe havens, providing an educational climate conducive to learning, free of alcohol, drugs, and violence. In order to improve school climates, correlates of violent behaviors in school settings must be identified. In a study conducted by Ellickson, Soner, and McGuigan (2004), correlates of school violence were identified among 17 and 18 year old seniors and students that had dropped out of school. Participants represented a diverse group from across the country, varying in socioeconomic status, race, and ethnic composition. Data derived from questionnaires revealed the following correlates associated with violent youth in schools: weekly drinking, low academic orientation, problem drug use, cocaine use, drug selling, minor delinquency, dropping out of school, poor mental health, and early pregnancy (p. 2). Correlates for violent females were different from males in that "girls were two or three times more likely to suffer from poor mental health and to report having children" (p.2).

Other correlates of school violence pertain to gangs and levels of violence in the communities in which the schools are located. Most schools with high levels of violence are located in communities with economic deprivation and minimal adult supervision (Garbarino, 2008; Galand, Lecocq, & Philippot, 2007). Also, Garbarino (2008) argued that "over the past 25 years there has been a doubling of children and youth who have mental health and developmental adjustment problems severe and chronic enough to warrant professional intervention" (p. 3). In essence, long-term intervention strategies must be implemented to reduce youth violence and aggression in schools. These strategies must include solutions for strengthening and empowering families within the school community.

Conclusion

Whether a person believes there is a genetic predisposition towards violence and aggression, or a person believes that the acquisition of violence is the result of learned behavior influenced by environmental forces, our country is in a state of unrest plagued by violent youth. News reports from countries from all over the world indicate the quality of life in our communities, workplaces, and schools has been threatened, and people are traumatized. Neighborhood gangs that regulate guns and drug distribution have replaced unstable families, producing toxic environments. This toxicity has spread to the schools, where violent acts are a daily occurrence. Students are more afraid of other students than they are of the police, administration, and teaching staff. Blatant disrespect permeates classrooms where students verbally abuse each other and their teachers. There is more disorder in some classes than order. Violence prevention programs need to be implemented in schools at every grade level, so these behaviors can be eliminated because they prevent students from learning. Unfortunately, there are no immediate solutions to these problems unless we can modify the infrastructure of our basic family unit, eliminating economic deprivation facilitated by poverty and ignorance. The onset of aggression has been investigated, risk factors have been identified, and trajectories outlined in accordance with developmental pathways. Now that the diagnosis has been made, it is time for intervention strategies and remediation.

APPLICATION

SBSF 8230 Professional Practice and Human Development

Introduction

Recently, a pluralistic, diverse group of people re-examined their self-interests and collectively elected a new president of the United States of America. From the onset of his campaign, President Obama has suggested an educational plan that demands a revamping of the educational system to facilitate a world-class education for American students. In this post-modern era, a better educated work force is definitely a prerequisite in preparation to competing in this global economy; however, even though President Obama's education plan sounds good, it does not address how the deleterious effect of school violence is placing educational institutions in a crisis mode. Woodson (2007) stated that "school reform supporters do not seem to appreciate that fear is the real stumbling block to learning (p. 805). Woodson further stated, "The reality of this fear of violence and its impact on education is not fully appreciated by the well-intentioned education and public officials who concern themselves with the low-performance in our schools today" (p. 805). Schools are inundated with aggressive, violent youth who persist in disrupting the educational process on a daily basis, making it impossible to maintain a learning environment conducive to raising academic achievement. Within school building, the school culture has been infiltrated by the street culture, and students and school personnel feel no safer in schools than they do on the streets (Woodson, 2007). These youth victimize classroom teachers, utilizing profane, obscene language and gestures, along with threats of physical violence and damage to their personal property. These youth continue to create disorder outside of the school building, extending into the community, compromising the safety of students. According to Gottfredson, Payne, and Gottfredson (2005), "youth are at elevated risk for victimization when they are in school or on the way to and from school" (p. 413). The *Center for the Study and Prevention of Violence*(2007) provided statistical data supporting Gottfredson et al. (2005) and stating that for every 1,000 students in a school, 5.5 per cent of students reported that they did not go to school because they felt unsafe at school, or on their way to or from school. Additional data from the 2007 National Crime Victimization Survey (NCVS) suggested that very little has changed since 2005 and that, "36 percent of all serious, violent crimes against 12 to 18 year olds (e.g. those including rape, sexual assault, robbery, or aggravated assault) occurred during school or on the way to and from school" (p. 2). However, the majority of the incidents involving students derive from disputes over property, romantic interests, or gang related bullying (Borg, 2009). These types of incidents are most common in high schools and post-secondary institutions. Thus, there are many factors contributing to aggression and violence in schools. Chen (2008) associates high numbers of school violence with urban schools located in poor communities. Current school practices also contribute to aggression and violence when they fail to identify and track high-risk students, implement ineffective intervention strategies, and fail to improve the overall school climate which is poor.

    This application project will contribute to the body of knowledge needed to address these problems by exploring the relevancy of school climate and current best practices utilized in successful school-based programs, as well as examining underlying rationales and analyzing a current school-based violence intervention program utilized today.

School Climate

School climate is synonymous to the organizational climate of a business, "encompassing a wide variety of school-level factors such as leadership, classroom instruction, classroom management, the physical surroundings, and the nature and tone of relationships therein" (Marzano, 2003, p. 60). According to Chen (2008), school climate is "a key factor in studying school process and school effect of student behavior and achievement" (p. 303). It is the overall environment of a school, including the physical or structural component of the building, characterized most importantly by a school's culture and the relationships, social and professional, between staff, students, and the administration. The National School Climate Council (2009) noted that a sustainable, positive school climate fosters youth development and learning necessary for a productive, contributing and satisfying life in a democratic society. This climate includes norms, values and expectations that support people feeling socially, emotionally, and physically safe. People are engaged and respected. Students, families, and educators work together to contribute to a shared school vision. Educators model and nurture attitudes that emphasize the benefits and satisfaction gained from learning. Each person contributes to the operations of the school and the care of the physical environment.

Today, formal and informal assessment tools are utilized to measure school climate such as the Charles F. Kettering Ltd. (CFK) School Climate Profile (2002) that is administered to students, teachers, and administrators. This tool measures levels of morale, trust, respect, and opportunity. Also, Freiberg's (1998) School Climate Survey is widely used and examines the specific areas of " order and discipline, parent involvement, fairness, achievement, motivation, student interpersonal relationships, student-teacher relationships, and the sharing of resources" (Hayes, Emmons, & Corner, 1993, p. 2). An informal assessment that administrators use is described by McKay (2000) as the "bathroom test". McKay (2000) suggested that school bathrooms are the most reliable indicators of a school's climate. If there are clean floors, ample soap, and paper towels, these factors are a sign of a healthy school climate. Old graffiti on walls, dirty floors, traces of cigarette smoke, no doors on stalls, and no tissue or soap are indicators of a poor school climate and probably that students are afraid of utilizing the facilities. Studies have indicated that school climate is the major variable that influences disorder in schools and is directly associated with levels of violence (Fein, Vossekull, Pollack, Borum, Medeleski, & Reddy, 2002; Gottfredson et al., 2005; Phaneuf, 2006; Chen, 2008). As levels of disorder and violence increase in school settings, students' levels of fear also increase. Students realize their school environment is unsafe, and some of the adults they rely upon for protection are incapable of assisting them, because they are incapable of assisting themselves. Students witness teacher victimization by disorderly youth who are removed temporarily, only to return to the scenes of their crimes and repeat them. When the parents of these disorderly youth are contacted, they act as if they are the ones being victimized, offering no support to the teachers. Teachers eventually become disillusioned with an educational system in which they advocate for students daily, but when they require assistance, this system fails to provide support. Consequently, they began to ignore the bullying, name-calling, and shoving that they observe between students, because they feel powerless to facilitate any lasting changes without the support of administrators and parents, who refuse to acknowledge that these anti-social behaviors are precursors to serious conflicts. This is the beginning of teacher disengagement. Teachers begin to question their effectiveness operating in an environment of fear. They will come to school to teach the curricula, but they refuse to volunteer for any student-centered activities beyond the scheduled dismissal time. Students also become frustrated because they fear other students more than they do the teachers. They find ways to protect themselves from the gang members and other disorderly youth by masquerading their fear behind facades of tough exteriors or bringing concealed weapons. The Center for the Study and Prevention of Violence reports that in 2007, 5.9% of students reported that they carried a weapon of some type to school for protection. This feeling of hopelessness and fear felt by teachers and students only serves to diminish the quality of an educational institution and to diminish the effectiveness of any academic rigor. Whether acts of aggression and violence, verbal or physical occur within a school building or its perimeters, the end result is the deterioration of a school's climate.

Sprague (2007) identified four areas that must be addressed by school officials to improve school climate and "reduce the risk factors that move schools in the direction of potential violence and reduced safety" (p.16). The first step to improving a school's climate is the identification of students who are at high risk for aggression and violence because students having prior behavior problems will negatively influence the culture of a school (Gottfredson et al., 2005). "Students with antisocial and violent behaviors present serious risks to the safety and climate of any school" (Sprague, 2007, p. 15). According to the Center for the Study and Prevention of Violence (CSPV) 2007 fact sheet, research characterized the following risk factors associated with aggressive-violent youth in school settings: "1. prior history of violence, 2. drug, alcohol, or tobacco use, 3. association with delinquent peers, 4. poor family functioning, 5. poor grades in school, 6. poverty in the community, 7. socially disorganized neighborhoods, 8. history of early aggressive behavior, 9. low I.Q, 10. poor behavioral control, 11. high emotional distress, and 12. antisocial beliefs and attitudes" (p. 2). Other student related factors associated with school-based violence are outlined in Chen's (2008) study based on his School Crime Model which suggested that "student demographics such as age, race, poverty, and socioeconomic status (SES) have been consistently found to be related to school crime and violence" (p. 302). Chem stated that schools that report high levels of violence have in attendance minority students whose eligibility for free and reduced lunches indicate family incomes that fall under the federal government guidelines for poverty. Student mobility is another related factor noted by Chen (2008) who argued that "schools with a higher level of student transience will have more crime" (p. 305). There are many students with mental health issues that have been diagnosed, and many students whose mental health issues are undiagnosed and who are incapable of functioning in an academic setting that add to the numbers of violent incidents in schools. Foster, Rollefson, Doksum, Noonah, Robinson, and Teich (2005) conducted a survey of 83,000 elementary, middle, and high school students across the United States, resulting in schools reporting that the number one health problem among all of the students were associated with their immediate families. The second and third highest problems among the male population were behavior problems associated with neurological disorders present at birth and problems with aggression or disruptive behavior. Among the female population, the second and third highest problems were anxiety, depression, and failure to adjust to new situations. All of these factors should be taken into consideration when school personnel are attempting to implement strategies to minimize school-based violence.

Reducing violence in schools is directly associated with building self-esteem through involvement (Calhoun, 2006; Chen, 2008). Calhoun (2006) noted that there are five characteristics necessary for the self-empowerment of youth:

1. *A lotus of control.* Youth should not feel like pawns in the hands of fate. They need to have a goal and recognize that their success or failure is in their own hands.
2. *A skill.* Whether it is through playing the violin, wrestling, or running a meeting, youth can point to a skill and feel confident in their abilities and secure about themselves.
3. *An adult who is always there.* No matter how severe the existential tornado becomes, youth must have a trusted, dependable, adult who supports them through the storms of life.
4. *Optimism.* Whether defined in a secular way ("I have hope for the future.") or theologically ("I am held in his hand."), youth must feel that their future is bright.
5. *Altruism.* Believing "I am my brother's keeper" or "I am my sister's keeper" gives young people a sense of responsibility for others beyond themselves. (p. 1)

These bonds are essential to building youth resilience, the characteristic that allows certain kids to make it against the odds (Calhoun, 2006). Building relationships between school personnel and students is essential to improving a school's climate. Studies reveal that schools that focus on student bonding promote individual student growth and student success (Sprague & Walker, 2005; Chen, 2008).

A sense of community must also be cultivated between students, teachers, and administrators to improve school climate. According to Fein, Vossekull, Pollack, Borum, Modzelski, and Reddy (2003), a safe school climate is one in which, "Each student feels that there is an adult to whom he or she can turn for support and advice if things get tough, and with whom that student can share his or her concerns openly and without fear of shame or reprisal" (p. 16). There is evidence that suggest a positive relationship between collaborative intervention approaches utilized by school administrative teams and the rate of school violence. According to Gottfredson et al. (2005), "communally organized schools experience less disorder and that the relationship between communal school organization and school disorder is partially mediated by student bonding" (p. 415).

Teachers are critical to a school's climate. They represent a major component due to their daily interactions with students. In reality, it is teachers, not administrators, who dictate how school policy is executed, because decision making in schools is really classroom based. Teachers ensure that students are knowledgeable regarding various events. Teachers distribute materials and convey messages from the administration to students in a timely manner. Administrators may formulate a school improvement plan, but without enthusiastic teachers who believe in the plan, it will never materialize. Teachers who work to make a difference in the lives of their students are a powerful force.

Sometimes school practices are complicit in cultivating unsafe climates. According to Sprague (2007), four school level predictors that contribute to school based violence and aggression are as follows: "1. failure to adequately supervise and monitor student behavior in classrooms and common areas, 2. unclear rules and expectations regarding appropriate behavior, 3. failure to effectively correct rule violations and reward adherence to them, and 4. failure to assist students from at-risk backgrounds to bond with the schooling process" (p.11). Studies by Gottfredson et al.(2005) concur "that schools that establish and maintain rules, effectively communicate clear expectations for behavior, consistently enforce rules, and provide rewards for rule compliance and punishments for rule infractions experience lower levels of victimization" (p. 418). Schools that do not promote clear guidelines for student conduct and students who claim that the rules are ambiguous tend to have more behavioral problems (D'Andrea, 2004; Chen 2008; Higgerson-Park et al., 2008).

The architectural design of the school building is an additional variable in determining levels of school-based aggression and violence. Sprague (2007) sited the following physical attributes: "1. heights of windows, 2. number of and types of entrances/exits, 3. location and design of bathrooms, 4. patterns of supervision, 5. traffic patterns and their management, 6. lightning, and 7. ratio of supervising adults to students" (p. 16). These aspects of a school's building design were altered decades ago by the Crime Prevention Through Experimental Design (CPTED) to allow for surveillance and so that schools would not look like maximum security penitentiaries. However, most schools are not equipped with this new technology. Sprague's (2007) four major sources of vulnerability to the safety of school settings have been briefly outlined above and are identified as follows: (1) characteristics of students enrolled, (2) nature of the neighborhood served by the school, (3) administrative and management practices of the school, and (4) design, use and supervision of school space. These four areas are consistent with current research studies (Fein, et al., 2003; Gottfredson, 2005; and Chen, 2008).

Legal Issues Supporting Safe Schools

Legal issues pertaining to safe schools have their origins in the United States Constitution. All citizens, including students, are endowed with inalienable rights provided by this legal document that school administrators must maintain. "All disciplinary action must respect the constitutional and statutory rights of the pupil" (Hamlin-Fish Institute, 2009, p. 5). Legal protections for students are provided under the First, Fourth, Fifth and Fourteenth Amendments. The First Amendment deals with freedom of expression, the Fifth Amendment protects students against self- incrimination, the Fourth Amendment protects students against illegal search and seizure, and the Fourteenth Amendment protects students against deprivation of liberty and property constituting equal protection and due

process under the law. Students who are accused of a minor school infraction (i.e. less than a 10-day suspension) must receive oral or written notice that explains the reasons. They have a right to tell their side of the story, and they must be given advanced warning regarding school rules and their consequences. The school discipline code must be clear, concise, and not ambiguous. Students who are accused of committing serious infractions requiring more than 10-day suspensions are entitled to the following: "1. notice of the disciplinary action given to students and parents preferably in writing, specifying the reason for action, 2. right to appeal decision in a fair, impartial hearing by school board, and superintendent; 3. facts of the case are evaluated independently, 4. the right to be represented by legal counsel, 5. reasonable time to prepare for hearing, 6. opportunity to review evidence against themselves, 7. the right to record proceedings, 8. hearing must be based on substantial evidence, 9.opportunity to examine witnesses against the student, 10. opportunity to present evidence and witnesses on the student's behalf" (Hamilton-Fish Institute, 2009, p. 8). If the student is a special education student, the Individuals with Disabilities Education Act (I.D.E.A.) revised disciplinary policies in 2004 so that misconduct may be considered a result of their disability if the following occurs: 1. the conduct was caused by the disability, 2. the conduct had a direct or substantial relation to the disability, 3. the conduct was the direct result of the schools' failure to implement the student's Individualized Education Plan (I.E.P.). In the latter case, the school will be out of compliance and subject to a lawsuit. However in the majority of cases, the courts understand a school's need for safety and usually sides with the school and not the perpetrator.

School-Based Violence Prevention Programs

In order to decrease levels of aggressive behaviors and violence in school settings, school-based violence prevention programs were initiated. These programs that promote school safety are a direct result of a publication titled *The Threat Assessment,* developed by the United States Secret Service in response to perpetrators who victimized public officials (Fein, Vossekuil, & Hilden, 1995). Following the school shootings at Columbine and Arkansas, Reddy, Borum, Berglund, Vossekuil, Fein, and Modzeleski (2001) suggested that *The Threat Assessment* should be utilized in schools. Therefore, in a combined report, the Federal Bureau of Investigation, the Secret Service, and the Department of Education also recommended that this document be utilized which eventually led to federal funding of the Safe Schools/ Healthy Students Initiative to facilitate the implementation of comprehensive school-based violence prevention programs. In 2002, under the NCLB Act, violence prevention program guidelines were revised and had to adhere to specific criteria and be empirically based. Armstrong and Webb (2006) suggested that these criteria should be modified because schools were unable to select the appropriate school-based violence intervention programs that addressed their specific school needs, due to a lack of planning. Thus, Armstrong and Webb (2006) formulated a plan that could be utilized by school personnel to assist in the selection and implementation of empirically based programs. Their systematic approach was utilized in a pilot program with three schools in Chicago, Illinois Jones Elementary School, Smith Middle School, and Johnson High School, consisting of five members from each school. The program focused on the following four training modules: (a) vision and goals, (b) needs assessment, (c) objectives and action plan, and (d) evaluating implementation and outcomes. Results indicated that the identification process was successful; however, the implementation was faulty. The NCLB Act guidelines interfered with daily curriculum practices, and some of the team members were not as enthusiastic or committed during the implementation phase as others. Armstrong and Webb (2006) stated, "During the pilot test, it became clear that the resource demands associated with meeting testing requirements eroded the ability of team members and their colleagues to fully invest themselves in a process with the potential to reduce violence in their schools (p. 92).

One of the problems facing school personnel because of the mandates of the NCLB Act was the requirement that school-based intervention programs provide evidence that they were grounded in scientifically based research and could supply data that programs could reduce aggression, violence, and illegal drug use. In response to this challenge, a meta-analysis was conducted by Park-Higgerson, Perumean-Chaney, Bartolucci, Grimley, and Singh (2008), utilizing 26 randomized control trial (RCT) school-based violence prevention programs to determine their viability in reducing aggressive and violent behaviors in school settings. Park-Higgerson et al. (2008) hypothesized that successful programs were characterized by the following five factors: (1) the application of theory, (2) the type of program such as universal or selective, (3) the number of programs such as single or multiple approach interventions, (4) the characteristics of the target population, and (5) the type of instructor, such as the use of specialists" (p. 466). The authors hypothesized that when a school-based intervention program's theoretical framework is inherited in its design, implementation, and interpretation, the program appears to exhibit more validity. The theory-based programs were more effective in decreasing violent behaviors than non-theory based programs. Park-Higgerson et al. (2008) argued that these school-based intervention programs should focus on high-risk students rather than a universal approach, only working with students whose behaviors required intervention. Programs that applied multiple approaches rather than single approaches, including participation from parents, peers, and the community, were more effective than single approaches that focused only on the perpetrator. These programs should be initiated with children rather than teenagers because children are more malleable. Also, Park-Higgerson et al. (2008) believed that professionals should come into the schools and administer these programs, not classroom teachers. Teachers are already overwhelmed, and adding an additional program to teach would compromise the effectiveness of the program. Higgerson et al. (2008) concluded that between the five indicators "there was no significant difference between interventions" (p. 465); however, all indicators had a positive affect in reducing aggression and violence.

    There are many viable school-based violent prevention programs utilized today, but the most effective ones appear to originate from behavioral theory. According to the Crisis Prevention Institute (2009), problem behavior continues to occur because it is consistently followed by the child getting something positive or escaping something negative. By focusing on the contexts and outcomes of the behavior, it is possible to determine the functions of the behavior, make the problem behavior less effective and efficient and make the desired behavior more functional. It involves changing systems, altering environments and teaching new skills (CrisisPrevention, 2009, ¶ 2). One program, the Schoolwide Positive Behavior Support (SWPBS) described by Osher, Dwyer, and Jackson (2002) and Sprague and Golly (2004) is a school-based program that focuses on preventing minor and serious behavior, "based on the assumption that when faculty and staff in a school actively teach and acknowledge expected behavior, the proportion of students with serious behavior problems will be reduced and the schools overall climate will improve" (p.15). The program focus is to "implement and sustain an organized school-wide system for behavior support and teaching social behavior which are the foundations for effective prevention" (p. 16). The theoretical framework for the program is based on the principles of behavior analysis and consists of three major components: (1) prevention, (2) multi-tiered support, and (3) data-based decision making. As of 2007, SWPBS was operating in 3,500 schools in various schools in the United States.

Another program that is widely used in the Chicago Public Schools is the Nonviolent Crisis Intervention Training Program. This Crisis Prevention Institute sponsors this program. The Executive Director of Research and Development for the Crisis Prevention Institute is Dr. Boardman, an experienced educator and administrator who has dedicated his life to devising strategies to assist educators with managing unmanageable students within schools. Dr. Boardman is an internationally acclaimed behavior management specialist and offers suggestions to educators that can be found in his pamphlet *10 Tips for Crisis Prevention.* Dr. Boardman and The Crisis Prevention Institute currently work with schools implementing the Nonviolent Crisis Intervention Training Program. The Crisis Prevention Institute is an international organization established in 1980 that "provides safe behavior management best practices and innovative resources to professionals around the world who are committed to creating safe and respectful work environments" (www.crisisprevention.com). This program is based on the theoretical framework of Positive Behavioral Support (PBS) that is founded on behavioral theory. Positive Behavioral Support (PBS) is an "empirically validated, function-based approach to eliminate challenging behaviors" (CPI, 2009, p. 2). Their goal is to enhance the quality of life by teaching its participants appropriate social skills in place of challenging behaviors. The program deals with manipulation of environmental variables (i.e. physical settings), tasks, curriculum, and individualized reinforcement. According to Sugai (2002), the five major components of the program are as follows: "1. prevention or a focused continuum of support, 2. proactive instructional approaches to teaching and improving social behaviors, 3. conceptually sound and empirically validated practices, 4. systems change to support effective practices, and 5. data-based decision making" (p. 130). The program utilizes a web-based discipline tracking system identified as the School Wide Information System (SWIS). Its purpose is to assist school personnel in designing school-wide and individual student interventions based on data. The primary elements of SWIS are that they are web based and easily accessible so that school personnel are able to submit data and generate reports in a timely manner and it can be a reliable tool in the decision making process. The Nonviolent Crisis Intervention Training Program (CPI, 2008) is directly aligned with PBS in 14 areas. Below is their alignment table.

Table 1

PBS Concept, Premise, or Strategy	Nonviolent Crisis Intervention Training
PBS is a broad, comprehensive approach which includes individual through systemic applications	Strategies, skills, interventions. And techniques taught within the Nonviolent Crisis Intervention training program can be used by individual staff members as well as by a team of responders. Implementation of the program's ongoing Training

	Process is designed to achieve culture change throughout an organization.
Used in many different settings.	More than 5.4 million people around the world have participated in Nonviolent Crisis Intervention training since 1980 in settings that include schools, hospitals, residential care, mental health facilities, human service organizations, security companies, corrections, law enforcement, and many other types of programs and organizations.
Prevention focus (primary, secondary, and tertiary levels.	The Nonviolent Crisis Intervention program produces outcomes in all three prevention categories: Decreasing the number of new cases of problem behavior. Decreasing the number of existing cases through specialized supports for "at-risk" individuals. Decreasing the intensity, duration, or frequency of complex long standing behaviors that put an individual at risk for significant emotional and social failure.
Collaborative team-driven approach, implemented by all parties involved.	CPI's programs support a collaborative approach to crisis de-escalation. Team intervention strategies are discussed for both verbal de-escalation and physical intervention. As part of the staff debriefing process outlined in the Post-prevention unit, team members

	discuss the successes and challenges they faced and plan to strengthen their team response for the future.
Person-centered plans that are function-based.	Person-centered approaches and language are taught throughout the Nonviolent Crisis Intervention training program. The CPI Crisis Development Model, as a foundation for the course, identifies an individual approach to behavior levels and staff attitudes to de-escalate the crisis by focusing on the "why" behind the "what" of behavior. As each unit unfolds to support the model, personalized supports are discussed. When discussing limit setting, there is a focus on setting limits around the function of the behavior rather than the form of the behavior. Finally, the Post-prevention process taught in Unit X provides structure for the staff to work cooperatively with the individual who experienced crisis to make a new plan for future behavior.
Data-based decision making (collection of the A-B-C-S). Exploration of the variables affecting, triggering, or maintaining a person's behaviors.	Unit V of the course explores various examples and types of antecedents or setting events that would "trigger" or set the stage for certain behaviors to occur. In addition, the relationship between behaviors and consequences is explored. Data collection is most specifically addressed as one of the CPI Coping Model components (Orient to the facts).

Teach new skills and positively reinforce pro-social behaviors.	Skill building is most clearly addressed in the section on limit setting. This section's focus is on teaching self-management of one's own behavior and learning how to make a positive choice.
Assess and modify the environment to make problem behaviors less likely.	Making environmental changes is one of the ways a staff member can provide support to an individual in crisis. This concept is explored throughout the program. Examples of this are found in the exploration of providing support to an individual displaying anxious behavior; in the isolating of an individual at the defensive level and redirecting the individual to a different environment, and in the exploration of how the environment may serve as a precipitant to acting-out behavior as discussed in Unit V.
Awareness that consequences (natural or stated) and staff responses can maintain a behavior.	The concept of the Integrated Experience, how staff's behaviors and attitudes affect the behaviors and attitudes of the individual in crisis, is a fundamental underpinning of the course. In addition, further discussions on limit setting assist staff with setting clear, reasonable, and enforceable limits that won't reinforce the negative behavior (intentionally or unintentionally).
Functional Behavior Assessment (FBA) is the	The components of the CPI COPING Model correlate

basis of Behavior Intervention Plan development and improves the effectiveness and efficiency of the intervention.	closely to the steps involved in an FBA. The steps serve as tools to use within the FBA process. The program explores how good Postvention efforts can enhance prevention efforts.
Analysis of behavioral patterns. Premise that human behavior is functional, predictable, and changeable.	An essential part of the CPI COPING Model is to look for patterns or antecedents in a person's behavior and to look for patterns in the staff responses—positive and negative, individually, and as a group. Debriefing exists to break the cycle of problematic behavior and negotiate an acceptable alternative that corresponds to the behavior's function. Using the debriefing process, patterns are explored and a behavior change process is negotiated.
If necessary to ensure safety and rapid de-escalation of the individual's behavior, crisis management procedures and criteria for their use are determined. Training and resources needed to ensure implementation of the Behavior Intervention Plan are made available to the team.	Nonviolent Crisis Intervention training builds confidence and competence among staff, improves communication and consistency in staff responses, reflects policy, and minimizes risks for all involved in the crisis moment.
Belief that behavior is a form of communication.	This belief underlies the foundation unit of the Nonviolent Crisis Intervention program, the CPI Crisis Developmental Model. This premise is also looked at in the units on nonverbal, paraverbal, and verbal

	communication in terms of both a staff member's behavior and that of the individual being served. Emphatic Listening is another area where staff are encouraged to "listen to the behaviors" and focus not only on facts but feelings and what might be the underlying message the person is attempting to communicate.
Outcome of its use is increased quality of life.	The purpose and philosophy of the Nonviolent Crisis Intervention training program is to provide for the best possible Care, Welfare< Safety< and Security of everyone involved in a crisis situation. This is achieved through appropriate prevention efforts and intervening at the earliest possible point when a crisis does occur. Through Postvention with the individual who experienced the crisis and among the intervention team responding is essential for achieving this outcome as well.

Crisis Prevention Institute, Inc. (2009).

This program employs a systematic method for modifying behavior based on a theoretical framework.

Action Plan to Improve School Climate

Fein et al. (2008) designed an action plan to be utilized by school leaders to facilitate a climate of safety. The plan is characterized by the following criteria:

"1. *Assess the school's emotional climate.* Distributing surveys and conducting face-to-face interviews, all of those qualitative methodologies, should be utilized to assess the school's climate. Stakeholders, especially students are the captured participants. 2. *Emphasize the importance of listening in schools.* Carl Rogers stressed the importance of listening in his therapeutic sessions. Respectful listening between students, teachers, and the administration should be ongoing to maintain the lines of open communication. A school with a culture of two-way listening will encourage and empower students to have the courage to break the ingrained code of silence. 3. *Take a strong, but caring stance against the code of silence.* Silence leaves people hurt unexposed and unacknowledged. Communication is the key to unlocking the doors to facilitate a dialogue with your young person. 4. *Work actively to change the perception that talking to an adult about a student contemplating violence is considered snitching.* A friend may save a life by reporting a student's pain. 5. *Find ways to stop bullying.* Teachers should address bullying, not ignore it. It creates a climate of fear and fosters disrespect. 6. *Empower students by involving them in planning, creating, and sustaining a culture of safety and respect.* Alienation is never good for students. A sense of community should be the goal. Community service projects serve to ensure students are productively engaged. 7. *Ensure that every student feels that he or she has a trusting relationship with at least one adult at school.* Every student in a school should have one adult he/she interacts with on a daily basis. The author stated, "Trusting adults and students are the products of quality connections, interactions and communications" (p.76). 8. *Create mechanisms for developing and sustaining safe school climates.* A mechanism for developing and sustaining safe school climates should serve as a vehicle for planning and monitoring the climate and culture of the school. 9. *Be aware of physical environments and their effects on creating comfort zones.* Building structure, facility safety plans lighting space, and architecture, among other physical attributes of educational institutions can contribute to whether a school environment feels safe. 10. *Emphasize an integrated systems model.* People support most what they had genuine input in creating. This requires the difficult but necessary task of bringing all of the stakeholders to the table. 11. *All climates of safety ultimately are local.* Many local features contribute to the creation of a culture and climate of safety. This includes the open door policy of the principal, people in the community, parents, and law enforcement personnel(pp. 75-76). All of the items covered in this *a*ction plan by Fein et al. (2007) are critical components in creating at atmosphere in which students thrive and excel.

Conclusion

There was a time, not so long ago, that public schools did not resemble maximum security prisons with metal-detectors and security guards at the end of every corridor. Even though Johnny could not read, he did not walk the around the school using profanity and victimizing teachers and his peers. There were always gangs, but they did not shoot innocent children as they played in their front yards. Drive-by shootings were unheard of because gang members could not afford cars, and they did not have essential commodities to sell. The world has changed, but some things still remain the same. Every student needs to feel that people are concerned about his or her welfare and that he or she is not just a statistic passing through the hall of academia. Teachers need to feel valued for the work they perform, because it is not just a paycheck when teachers spend more time completing tasks for work than they do at home. All school personnel require respect, praise, recognition, encouragement, and genuine positive regard, because they are human beings that take their jobs home with them daily. From the principal to the cafeteria manager to the custodians and the bus drivers, these people are caregivers of students who face daily challenges within their specific schools. The most important challenge educators' face is building relationships between students and school personnel in order to cultivate a sense of community, so youth can be reclaimed and school climates can be improved. Building a sense of community is difficult without parents and community partners who are not active participants in the educational process. However, educators have no other choice than to begin with the school climate. Research studies indicate that a positive school climate is directly correlated with a school's ability to increase and maintain academic excellence and to decrease levels of aggression and violence.

REFERENCES

Alink, L.., Mesman, J., Zeijl, J., Stolk, M., Juffer, F., & Koot, H., et al. (2006). The early childhood aggression curve: Development of physical aggression in 10-to-50-month old children. *Child Development, 77*(4), 954-966.

Anderson, M. (2001. School-associated violent deaths in the United States, 1994-1999. *Journal of the American Medical Association, 286,* 2695-2702.

Anhalt, K., Telzrow, C., & Brown, C. (2007). Maternal stress and emotional status during the perinatal period and childhood adjustment. *School Psychology Quarterly, 22*(1), 74-90.

Armstrong, T. & Webb, V. (2006). The school-based violence prevention planning program: A pilot test. *Journal of School Violence, 5*(4), 79-98.

Bandura, A. (1969). *Principles of behavior modification.* New York: Holt, Rinehart, & Winston.

Bandura, A. (1973). *Aggression: A social learning analysis.* Englewood Cliffs, NJ: Prentice-Hall.

Bandura, A. (1977). *Social learning theory.* Upper Saddle River, NJ: Prentice-Hall.

Bandura, A. (2001). Social cognitive theory: A genetic perspective. *Annual Review of Psychology Today; 52* (1), 1-26.

Bandura, A. (1969). *Principles of behavior modification.* New York: Holt, Rinehart & Winston.

Bandura, A. (2004). Broadening the cognitive, motivational, and socio-structural scope of theorizing about gender development functioning. *Psychological Bulletin, 130*(5), 691-701.

Bandura, A., Barbaranelli, C., Caprara, G., & Pastorelli, C. (2001). Self-efficacy beliefs as shapers of children's aspirations and career trajectories. *Child Development, 72*(1), 187-207.

Bandura, A., Barbaranelli, C., Caprara, G., Gerbino, M., & Pastorelli, C. (2003). Role of affective self-regulatory efficacy in diverse spheres of psychosocial functioning. *Child Development, 74*(3), 769-782.

Beaver, K., DeLisi, M., Wright, J., Vaughn, M. (2009). Gene environment interplay and delinquent involvement: Evidence of direct, indirect, and interactive effects. *Journal of Adolescent Research, 24*(2), 147-168.

Blanck, G. (1984). *The life and work of Vygotsky*. In G. Blanck (Ed.) Vygotsky: Memory and actuality. Buenos Aires: Stokoe.

Bonari, L., Pinto, N., Ahn, E., Einarson, A., ASteiner, M., Koren, G. (2004). Perinatal risks of untreated depression during pregnancy. *Canadian Journal of Psychiatry, 9*(11), 726-734.

Bozhovich, L. (2004). L. Vygotsky's historical and cultural theory and its significance for contemporary studies of the psychology of personality. *Journal of Russian* and *East European Psychology, 42 (4)*, 20-34.

Brennan, P., Hall, J. Bor, W., Najman, J., & Williams, G. (2003). Integrating biological and social processes in relation to early-onset persistent aggression in boys and girls. *Developmental Psychology, 39*(2), 309-323.

Brook, D., Zhang, C., Rosenberg, G., & Brook, J. (2006). Maternal cigarette smoking during pregnancy and child aggressive behavior. *The American Journal on /American Academy of Psychiatrists in Alcoholism and Addictions, 15*(6), 450-456.

Bruner, J. (1977). *The relevance of education*. New York: Norton.

Calhoun, J. (2006). Proven paths to violence prevention. *Reclaiming Children and Youth, 15,* 19-23.

Chen, G. (2008). Communities, students, schools, and school crime: A confirmatory study of crime in U.S. high schools. *Urban Education, 43*(3), 301-318.

Chomsky, N. (2006). *Language and mind.* Cambridge, MD: Cambridge University Press.

Crisis Prevention Institute (2009). *Program alignment.* Chicago, IL: CPI.

D'Andrea, M. (2004). Comprehensive school-based violence prevention training: A developmental-ecological training model. *Journal of Counseling and Development, 82*(3), 277-283.

Davidson, R., Putnam, K., Larson, C., Lee, L., & Coccaro, E. (2000). Dysfunction in the neural circuitry of emotion regulation-a possible prelude to violence. *Science,* 591-595.

Demorest, A. (2005). *Psychology's grand theorists: How personal experiences shaped professional ideas.* Mahwah, NJ: Lawrence.

Dragon, N. (2006). Pressure rising against violence. *Australian Nursing Journal, 14*(5), 21-24.

Ewen, R.B. (2003). *An introduction to theories of personality.* Mahwal, NJ: Lawrence Erlbaum Associates.

Feder, J., Levant, R., & Dean, J. (2007). Boys and violence: A gender-informed analysis *Professional Psychology: Research & Practice, 38*(4), 385-391.

Fein, R., Vossekuil, B., & Holden, G., Pollack, W., Borum, R., Modzeleski, Reddy, M. (2008). Threat assessment in schools: An approach to prevent targeted violence. *National Institute of Justice: Research in Action, 1-7.* Available at http://www.secretservice.gov/ntac.htm.

Ferreiro, E. (2001). On the links between equilibration causality and prise de conscience' `in Piaget's theory. *Human Development, 9(4)*, 214-219.

Flanagan, K., Bierman, K., & Kam, C. (2003). Identifying at-risk children at school entry: The usefulness of multibehavioral problem profiles. *Journal of Clinical Child and Adolescent Psychology, 32*(3), 396- 407.

Forbes, E., Shaw, D., Fox, N., Cohn, J., Silk, J., & Kovace, M. (2006). Maternal depression, child frontal asymmetry and child affective behavior as factors in child behavior problems. *Journal of Child Psychology and Psychiatry, 47*(1), 79-87.

Gottfredson, G., Gottfredson, D., Payne, A., & Gottfredson, N. (2005). School climate predictors of school disorder: Results from a national study of delinquency prevention in schools. *Journal of Research, Crime, and Delinquency, 42*(4), 412-444.

Grinberg, I., Dawkins, M., Dawkins, M., & Fullilove, C. (2005). Adolescents at risk for violence: An initial validation of the life challenges questionnaire and risk assessment index. *Adolescence, 40*(159*)*, 573- 599.

Higgerson-Park, H., Perumean-Chaney, S., Bartolucci, A., Grimley, D., and Singh, K. (2008). The evaluation of school-based violence prevention programs: A meta-analysis. *Journal of School Health, 78*(9), 465-479.

Hodgins, S., Cree, A., Alderton, J., and Mak, T. (2008). From conduct disorders to severe mental illness: Associations with aggressive behaviour, crime and victimization. *Psychological Medicine, 38,* 975-987.

Jaffe, S., Belsky, J., Harrington, H., Caspi, A., & Moffitt, T. (2006). When parents have history of conduct disorder: How is the caregiving environment affected? *Journal of Abnormal Psychology, 115*(2), 309-319.

Kail, R. V. (2004). Cognitive development includes global and domain-specific processes. *Merrill-Palmer Quarterly, 50(4)*, 445.

Kaufman, P. (2000). *Indicators of school crime and safety*. U.S. Department of Education (NCES 2001-017): Washington, D.C.

Kozulin, A. (1986). The concept of activity in Soviet psychology: Vygotsky, his disciples and critics. *American Psychologist, 4*(3), 264-274.

Lier, P., & Crijnen, A. (2005). Trajectories of peer-nominated aggression: Risk status, predictors and outcomes. *Journal of Abnormal Child Psychology, 33* (1), 99-112.

Linnet, K., net, K., Obel, C., Bonde, E., Thomsen, P., Secher, N., Wisborg, K., & Henriksen, T.(2006). Cigarette smoking during pregnancy and hyperactive-distractible preschooler's: A follow-up study. *Acta Pediatrica, 95*, 694-700.

Marzano, R. (2003). *What works in schools: Translating research into action.* Alexandria, VA: Association for Supervision and Curriculum Development.

Moffit, T. (2005). The new look of behavioral genetics in developmental psychopathology: Gene environment interplay in antisocial behaviors. *Psychological Bulletin, 131*(4), 553-554.

Moll, L. (Ed.). (2004). *Vygotsky and Education: Instructional implications and applications of sociohistorical psychology.* New York: Cambridge University Press.

Piaget, J. (1968). *Six psychological studies.* New York: Random House.

Piaget, J. (1969). *The psychology of the child.* New York: Basic Books.

Piaget, J.(1969).*The mechanisms of perception.* London: Rutledge & Kegan Paul.

Piaget, J. (2004). *The language and thought of the child.* New York: Marjorie & Ruth Gabain.

Pugliese, J. & Tinsley, B. (2007). Parental socialization of child and adolescent physical activity: A meta-analysis. *Journal of Family Psychology, 21*(3), 331-343.

Retz, W., Retz-Junginger, P., Supprian, T., Thome, J., & Roster, M. (2004). Association of serotonin transporter promoter gene polymorphism with violence: Relation with personality disorders, impulsivity, and childhood ADHD psychopathology. Psychiatry Research, 158(2), 123-131.

Schedrovitsky, G. (1982). Comment. In K. Levitin, *One is not born a personality* (pp. 59-63). Moscow: Progress.

Sprague, J. R. & Walker, H. M. (2005). *Safe and healthy schools: Practical prevention strategies.* New York: Guilford Press.

Tremblay, R. (2004). Decade of behavior distinguished lecture: Development of physical aggression during infancy. *Infant Mental Health Journal, 25(5)*, 399-407.

Tremblay, R., Nagin, D., Seguin, J., Zoccolillo, M., Zelazo, P., Boivin, M., et al. (2004). Physical aggression during early childhood: Trajectories and predictors. *Pediatrics,* 114(1), e43-e50.

Van Der Veer, R. & Valsiner, J. (1994). *The Vygotsky reader.* Oxford, UK: Blackwell.

Vygodskaya, G. (1984). *Lev Semenovich Vigotskii.* In L. Moll (Ed.) Vygotsky, Cambridge, MA:MIT Press.

Vygotsky, L.S.(1962). *Thought and language.* (A. Kozulin (Ed.), Cambridge, MA:MIT Press.

Vygotsky, L.S. (1987). *The collected works of L. S. Vygotsky* (Vol. 1). New York: Plenum.

Vygotsky, L.S. (1978). *Mind in society.* Cambridge, MA: Harvard University Press.

Wertsch, J. (1985). *Vygotsky and the social formation of mind.* Cambridge, MA: Harvard University Press.

Printed in Great Britain
by Amazon